MW00943149

PRAY LIKE JESUS

What We Can Learn from the Six Recorded Prayers of Jesus

Robert L. Morris Jr.

This book is a work of non-fiction. Unless otherwise noted, the author and the publisher make no explicit guarantees as to the accuracy of the information contained in this book and in some cases, names of people and places have been altered to protect their privacy.

WestBow Press books may be ordered through booksellers or by contacting:

WestBow Press
A Division of Thomas Nelson & Zondervan
1663 Liberty Drive
Bloomington, IN 47403
www.westbowpress.com
1 (866) 928-1240

Because of the dynamic nature of the Internet, any web addresses or links contained in this book may have changed since publication and may no longer be valid. The views expressed in this work are solely those of the author and do not necessarily reflect the views of the publisher, and the publisher hereby disclaims any responsibility for them.

ISBN: 978-1-9736-6764-3 (sc)
ISBN: 978-1-9736-6766-7 (hc)
ISBN: 978-1-9736-6765-0 (e)

Library of Congress Control Number: 2019908998

Print information available on the last page.

WestBow Press rev. date: 7/15/2019

CONTENTS

Acknowledgements

Truth be told, I am the least likely person to ever write a book. I only read one book my entire high school career. I learned how to study in college, but I still think that Princeton Seminary got my application confused with someone else far more talented and deserving.

Yet now, after forty-six years of ministry, I am grateful for Charlie Scott and Lester Comee, who saw something in me while I was a college student and volunteer Young Life leader. They taught me how to love Jesus and to love the Church.

This book would not be possible if it were not for the encouragement of the leaders at First Presbyterian Church in Jacksonville, Florida, and to the Young Life Regional Staff in Florida. Each providing time and encouragement to finish the project.

Grateful for my sister, Judy, and brother-in-law, Chris, who so generously loaned me their mountain home more times than I can count to escape to work and think. Thankful for

Marilyn Thomas, my wonderful mother-in-law and first editor and proofreader.

Most of all, I am grateful for my two sons and daughters-in-law who believed in me and encouraged me. I am particularly grateful to my wife, Virginia, who is often described as the perfect minister's wife. And that she is. She is the best person I have ever known. I am blessed indeed.

Introduction

What do all Christians talk about and do very little of? Pray! Yes, prayer is the most talked-about subject in Christendom, but very few people regularly do it. Developing a prayer life for me was and is a journey. I came to faith at a Young Life weekend camp when I was fifteen. All I knew was that I was lost, and I gave myself to the Lord with all the maturity a fifteen-year-old could muster. Prayer, at that time, consisted of me telling God what to do to make me happy. That's all I thought prayer was.

Upon graduation from high school, I matriculated to the University of South Florida; coincidentally, Young Life had just placed a staff person in Tampa that same year. I got a call from John Smith (yes, his real name—he later married Dolly Pure, a sex education teacher). John was the new staff guy in Tampa, and he asked if I would like to become a volunteer song leader at a local Young Life club. Young Life had been so life-changing for me; I thought of this volunteer work as a thank you to the Lord for how Jesus Christ used Young Life to change my life.

Being a volunteer leader helped me mature a bit, but I still saw God as this cosmic Santa Claus—if I led a good, moral life, God would reward me with good things, and if I did bad things, God would rain plagues and infirmities into my life. In short, I believed God blesses good people and hammers the bad people of the world.

But deep down I was troubled. You see, my sister Barbara had Down syndrome. Was this birth defect a punishment for some sin? I wondered, How could God do this to my sister? What sin could she have committed before she was even born to deserve this? So here I was, a young Christian praying to the Cosmic Santa to reward me for my good life, yet deep down I knew my theology had huge holes in it and at times was even quite illogical.

My college career began with the thought of preparing for law school while giving as much time possible to being a volunteer Young Life leader. I dated Virginia Thomas (who became my future wife), and as I approached graduation, I was invited to join the Young Life staff. Neither Virginia nor I could imagine doing anything other than ministry at that time, so we said so long to the dream of being a lawyer (including the goals of a white Porsche and home on the beach) and welcome to an adventure of faith and ministry.

Virginia and I married in 1975. I joined the Young Life staff that same year, with a whopping salary of $640 per month (funds I had to raise). But within a few months, the guy who was my Young Life supervisor left Tampa to pursue other things. I was now the acting area director. No training, no money, no experience, but the Lord was faithful. I prayed for my leaders by name and the specific families we ministered to. I learned to pray for others and for the salvation of entire communities (and God did change people and even neighborhoods), but the prayers also changed me. It was the love I had for those I ministered to and alongside that compelled me to pray—this time not just for myself but for them. I was growing as a believer!

We loved being on staff, but after a decade, I felt a need to go still deeper with the Lord. So I applied to a number of seminaries, and in 1984, with Virginia and new son in tow, began my theological education at Princeton Theological Seminary. I had a great hope that seminary would allow me the time to plumb the depths of what it meant to follow Jesus and gain a more complete understanding of theology and the wonderful mysteries of God's Word. I remember the seminary president welcoming my incoming class by telling us that the academics were so demanding, half of us would not be there by Christmas. I was sure he was talking to me. After all, I was not a gifted student. But I learned a lesson that has proven true time and again: hard work beats natural ability every time—I survived, and by the end, I was thriving academically.

I graduated a few years later, and seminary prepared me to be a Presbyterian clergyman, but sadly, it didn't help grow my heart. I left seminary, knowing a lot more theology and church history but honestly not knowing any more about prayer than when I arrived.

But one nugget given to me by a professor has stuck with me over the years. He said, "Robert, you won't know what you're doing in ministry until you're at least fifty-five years old, and then you will have about fifteen years when you have hit your peek. Everything you do and learn before you are fifty-five is all preparation. Your peak is between fifty-five and seventy, and once you're over seventy, it's all up to the Lord and your health."

He was right. Over the last thirty years, the Lord has taught me a great deal about what it means to be a follower and how prayer is an integral part of any believer's daily life. So, after fifteen years of being on Young Life staff and twenty-six years serving three different Presbyterian churches, the Lord has moved me to share my prayer journey. I must confess that even though I believe with all my heart that a rich prayer life is essential to fulfilling Christ's call to serve, love, and lead, there were times that I struggled. Most people think women and men who serve in full-time ministry have all the time in the world to develop a spiritual life. The sad fact is, the demands of ministry, eighty-hour work weeks, human frailty, and regular crises can make "regular" prayer time a challenge. So I write this book not as an expert but as a fellow struggler.

I would also say without hesitation that developing a rich and vital prayer life is *the* chief spiritual struggle for all believers. Further, I am convinced that the reason churches are full of men and women who are spiritual pygmies (stunted in their spiritual growth) is that they have never developed a consistent prayer life. Many pew sitters are people who, somewhere in their lives, asked Christ to be their Savior but made him more of an advisor than Lord. Many who call Jesus their Savior are like the three-year-old I saw at a friend's swimming pool one afternoon. She (the three-year-old) stood on the first step of the pool, ankle deep, an inner tube around her waist, hanging on the metal handrail. Then she turned to her mother, who was keeping a watchful eye from her lounge chair, and yelled, "Look, Mom! I'm swimming!" She was ankle deep yet claimed to be all in.

Believers who don't develop a healthy prayer life are like that. We may belong to a church, even read our Bible every once in a while, and fire off a prayer when life goes all wrong, but make no mistake—most Christians are still only ankle deep in their faith; they are not all in. That kind of prayer life will not sustain us when the hurricanes of life hit.

Remember Jesus's parable of the man who built his house on sand and one who built it on rock? In that parable, Jesus didn't say, "Some will get storms and some won't." No, Jesus said that storms come to all (Matthew 7:24–27). As a minister, it is heartbreaking to see Christians, who are only ankle deep in their faith, crumble under the weight of life's storms. It doesn't have to be like that. Spiritual vitality begins with a foundation of prayer.

This short book is intended to be a simple spiritual how-to manual for those who do not have a vital prayer life but seek one. It is not intended to be an academic book as much as it is an epistle from a fellow believer who may have learned a few things in forty-one years of ministry. We will look at six prayers of Jesus, but we will intentionally not examine the Lord's Prayer in depth. The reason is simple: the Lord's Prayer contains valuable information on how disciples should pray, but this book is about how Jesus personally prayed. This book is not the destination but a directional sign. Jesus, and no other, is the destination.

CHAPTER 1

WHAT IS PRAYER?

THERE ARE MORE than six hundred prayers in the Bible, and all have something to teach us. But for our purpose, the most enlightening prayers are those of our Savior. In the pages ahead we will sit at the feet of Rabbi Jesus as he teaches us about prayer. Because Jesus often prayed alone, no one was present to record his actual words.[1] Therefore, these

[1] Here is a list of times Jesus prayed: (Luke 3:21–22) At his baptism. (Mark 1:35–36) In the morning before heading to Galilee. (Luke 5:16) After healing people. (Luke 6:12–13) Praying all night before choosing his twelve disciples. (Matthew 11:25–26) While speaking to the Jewish leaders. (John 6:11) Giving thanks to the Father before feeding five thousand. (Also see Matthew 14:19, Mark 6:41, Luke 9:16.) (Matthew 14:23) Before walking on water. (Also see Mark 6:46, John 6:15.) (Mark 7:31–37) While healing a

prayers are not in the New Testament. But some of Jesus's actual prayers (or prayer fragments) did get included in the Bible. That is no accident. Those prayers are gifts from God to teach us who Jesus is. Moreover, I believe the Holy Spirit placed them there to teach us how to pray like Jesus. Did you catch that? Yes, you and I can pray like Jesus! But before we begin to let Jesus teach us how to pray, there are a few questions that many believers have concerning prayer.

Question 1: Why did Jesus pray at all? Isn't Jesus, being God, just talking to himself?

I believe Jesus prayed for three primary reasons. First, Jesus

---

deaf and mute man. (Matthew 15:36) Giving thanks to the Father before feeding four thousand. (Also see Mark 8:6–7.) (Luke 9:18) Before Peter called Jesus "the Christ." (Luke 9:28–29) At the transfiguration. (Luke 10:21) At the return of the seventy. (Luke 11:1) Before teaching his disciples the Lord's Prayer. (John 11:41–42) Before raising Lazarus from the dead. (Matthew 19:13–15) Laying hands on and praying for little children. (Also see Mark 10:13–16, Luke 18:15–17.) (John 12:27–28) Asking the Father to glorify his name. (Matthew 26:26) At the Last Supper. (Also see Mark 14:22–23, Luke 22:19.) (Luke 22:31–32) Praying for Peter's faith when Satan asked to "sift" him. (John 17:1–26) Prayed for himself, his disciples, and all believers just before heading to Gethsemane. (Matthew 26:36–46) In Gethsemane, before his betrayal. (He prayed three separate prayers.). (Also see Luke 22:39–46, Mark 14:32–42.) (Luke 23:34) Right after being nailed to the cross, Jesus prayed, "Father, forgive them; for they know not what they do." (Matthew 27:46) While dying on the cross, Jesus cried out, "My God, my God, why hast thou forsaken me?" (Also see Mark 15:34.) (Luke 23:46) In his dying breath, Jesus prayed, "Father, into thy hands I commend my spirit. (Luke 24:30) Prayed a blessing on the bread before he ate with others after his resurrection. (Luke 24:50–53) He blessed the disciples before His ascension.

wanted to be an example to his followers. He knew that a vital prayer life is not optional. It is a basic building block for those who want to live faithful lives. Jesus wanted his disciples—and us today—to witness our Lord doing what he calls us to do. Jesus made prayer a priority. Jesus prayed regularly. Jesus prayed with passion. All these things were witnessed by those who followed Jesus, and it made a tremendous impact on those first disciples. They were men who were Easter people. They were transformed by the resurrection of our Lord and then launched the early church. How did these courageous believers achieve such faithfulness? They prayed like Jesus, and so can we.

Second, Jesus prayed because it gave him the spiritual strength to accomplish his mission. Colossians 2:9 tells us, "For in him the whole fullness of deity dwells bodily." Indeed, Jesus was fully God, but he was also fully human. The apostle Paul writes in Philippians 2:7, "but emptied himself, taking the form of a slave, being born in human likeness." So the human side of Jesus, who was both fully God and human, needed prayer just like we do. I have often thought of Jesus the night before his crucifixion in the garden of Gethsemane. The scriptures say he "threw himself onto the ground" and prayed to his heavenly Father that "this cup may pass." Jesus was in such agony, knowing what was before him, that three times he asked his Father to spare him from the cross (Matthew 26:39). Ultimately, Jesus surrendered to the will of his Father. I believe this prayer time with his Father was not a means of escape but a means to ready Jesus for the horror that was about to happen. Jesus needed prayer in his life too.

Finally, Jesus needed to pray because the Trinity (God, Son, and Holy Spirit) needs to communicate. Even today, Jesus is still praying for us. Three texts (Hebrews 7:25; Romans 8:34; 1 John 2:1) tell us that Jesus continues to intercede for us even today.

Question 2: Why should we pray?

We pray because Jesus told us to pray. Matthew 6:6 says, "But whenever you pray, go into your room and shut the door and pray to your Father who is in secret; and your Father who sees in secret will reward you." Notice Jesus doesn't say "if" you pray. Prayer is expected of all followers. But why?

Some have said that prayer is a kind of a spiritual therapy God established for his children. Others have said it is a way of lifting ourselves up to God (as if that were even possible). Still, others think prayer is like a cosmic wishing well. As I have previously stated, I treated God like a spiritual butler or Santa Claus. I tried to live a good life, but then I would give him my laundry list of things I wanted him to do so my life would be happy. My prayers focused on me and my wants, hopes, and needs. If a close friend had some important issue or upcoming event, I might mention my friend in my prayers, but probably 95 percent of my prayer time was all about me.

Now, don't misunderstand. I still believe that scripture teaches that we are to go to God with all our wants and desires—as a child would go to a parent. Recently, at the grocery store, I was waiting in a long checkout line. In front of me was a mom with a five-year-old daughter and a son who was two or three. As the line moved at glacier speed, that little boy must have asked his mom twenty-five times if he could have some candy. He would reach out from his seat in the shopping cart and attempt to grab a candy bar, and the mom would say no. That never slowed him down. He pulled M&M's from the shelf, and the mom said no. Then it was chewing gum. These requests went on for at least ten minutes. (I found myself praying for the sanity of that mom!)

As I watched this episode playing out before me, I realized I had been just like that little boy! For many years, that was how I prayed to my Lord. Then, as I knew Jesus more and trusted the Lord with more and more of my life, my prayer life matured. Yes, I still go to the Lord while sharing all aspects of my life, but my prayer goal has now shifted. I no longer pray to get God to fulfill my agenda, but I believe prayer is God's way to get me on his agenda.

Jesus told a parable about an unjust judge (Luke 18:1–8). In it was an unjust judge and a widow who had been wronged. This widow relentlessly came to the judge to ask for justice. Eventually, the judge grew tired of the widow's constant requests and gave her justice. At the end of the parable, Jesus said if an evil judge answers such requests, how much more will our Father in heaven respond to those he loves? The message here is that constant and repeated prayer is perfectly appropriate, yet I would argue that prayer is more than getting God to do something. It is to align our hearts with God's heart.

Do you remember the story of the transfiguration? Matthew tells us in the seventeenth chapter of his gospel that Jesus had invited Peter, James, and John to a mountaintop. The text says

Jesus was transfigured as if a thousand spotlights were shining on him. Both Moses and Elijah showed up and began to talk with Jesus.

This was a sacred moment; God was preparing Jesus for the cross and the redemption of the world. But what does Peter do? He is so preoccupied with his personal agenda that he breaks into this holy scene by asking if he should make some tents for Moses, Elijah, and Jesus.

Finally, God speaks. "This is my Son of whom I am well pleased; listen to him!" What God was saying to Peter was that he was so focused on himself that he was missing the profound event happening before his eyes.

I have to confess that my prayer life for many years was like that. I spent so much time focused on me and my wants that I often missed what God wanted to communicate to me.

So, at its core, we should pray like a child who shares his or her heart with a parent. But the goal is not to get something from God. The goal is to allow the Spirit of God to place within our hearts, minds, and souls the very will of God.

Question 3: What were Jesus's prayer habits?

In the days of Jesus's earthly ministry, all practicing Jews prayed three times a day. There is little doubt that Jesus too prayed those customary times, yet the Bible records Jesus praying only twenty-five times. It is only logical that there were many more times than that. It is clear that customary prayers, and prayers when Jesus was alone, were never recorded. Luke 5:16 tells us that Jesus prayed regularly. "But he would withdraw to deserted places and pray." Here we see that Jesus prayed alone, but we know he prayed with others as well.

In all the recorded prayers of Jesus, nowhere is a specific manner of prayer described. The scriptures show Jesus praying while standing, sitting, and lying face down on the ground. The Bible does not report that Jesus held his palms upward while he prayed. Nor did he always lift his hands to the heavens. It also does not say he always knelt. And there is no indication that he prayed at a specific time of day. Robert Velarde[2] reminds us of some key things we do know about Jesus's prayer life, such as the following:

- Jesus prayed for others. In Matthew 19:13, we read, "Then little children were being brought to him in order that he might lay his hands on them and pray."
- Jesus prayed with others. Luke 9:28 reads, "Now about eight days after these sayings Jesus took with him Peter and John and James, and went up on the mountain to pray."
- Jesus prayed alone. Luke 5:16 says, "But he would withdraw to deserted places and pray."
- Jesus prayed on the mountains. Luke 6:12 says, "Now during those days he went out to the mountain to pray."

---

[2] Robert Velarde is the author of *Conversations with C. S. Lewis* (InterVarsity Press), *The Heart of Narnia* (NavPress), and primary author of *The Power of Family Prayer* (National Day of Prayer Task Force). He studied philosophy of religion and apologetics at Denver Seminary and is pursuing graduate studies in philosophy at Southern Evangelical Seminary. http://www.focusonthefamily.com/faith/faith-in-life/prayer/learning-from-the-prayer-life-of-jesus.

- Jesus prayed repetitiously. In Matthew 26:39, Jesus asks three times not to face the cross. He also taught this principle of repetitious prayer in the parable of the judge and the persistent widow (Luke 18).
- Jesus taught his believers short prayers. In Matthew 6:9–13, Jesus taught the disciples the Lord's Prayer. It is a very short prayer, indeed.
- Jesus prayed for long periods of time. In Luke 6:12, Jesus "spent the night praying to God."
- Jesus prayed with passion. Hebrews 5:7 tells us: "In the days of his flesh, Jesus offered up prayers and supplications, with loud cries and tears, to the one who was able to save him from death, and he was heard because of his reverent submission."

When was the last time you wept as you prayed? Most of the time my prayers aren't filled with tears, yet sometimes I am overwhelmed by human suffering and the prayerful tears come. Not long ago I was in Jamaica on a mission trip. Our mission team was building a home for an elderly Jamaican couple and their disabled grandson. One day, while having lunch on the worksite, the special-needs boy approached one of our teammates and asked for his lunch—the boy was hungry. We all watched speechlessly as that team member gave his food to the boy.

Later that night, I prayed for those grandparents and that boy with special needs. I thought about this family who lived in filth—their old home was nothing more than walls made of cardboard and scrap wood with a mud floor, and I wondered what would ever happen to that boy. My heart broke, tears came, and I remembered the words of the prayer: "May the things that break the heart of Jesus break our hearts." That day it did. Jesus prayed with passion, and so should we.

I welcome the fact that Jesus demonstrated what a healthy prayer life looks like: one that is consistent, timely, and passionate. Let's keep digging.

CHAPTER 2

WHY BOTHER?

ONE OF THE defining stories for the nation of Israel is of Moses leading the Israelites out of Egypt. We all know the story: God sent Moses to Pharaoh to tell him to let the Israelites go, Pharaoh refused, and God used ten plagues to convince Pharaoh to change his mind. Following Passover, Pharaoh decided to let the Israelites pack up their belongings and head east to the Promised Land.

As the Israelites made their escape from slavery, Pharaoh, in a fit of rage and regret, changed his mind again and sent six hundred chariots to bring Moses and the ex-slaves back to Egypt. The Israelites encamped adjacent to the Red Sea; suddenly, they see Pharaoh and the chariots in hot pursuit.

The Israelites panicked and blamed Moses for what looked like would be a certain slaughter. Then God intervened, separating the waters of the Red Sea, making a way of escape.

I have always wondered what it must have been like for those Israelites crossing the Red Sea. Who could imagine that these ex-slaves would be, by the power of God, walking between walls of water suspended on each side of them and Pharaoh hot on their heels? My guess is that all those Israelites had some faith, or they wouldn't have set foot in the Red Sea in the first place.

After more than forty years of ministry, I have experienced two kinds of believers. One kind is someone who believes in God, but only to a point. They believe and trust God with parts of their lives, but not all. This kind of believer says, for example, that they believe in tithing yet never tithe. They trust God with their eternal soul but not their money. Their disobedience in tithing is rarely a financial issue. It is a spiritual one. They don't tithe because they are not certain the Lord will take care of them financially, as he promises. They clutch on to those resources with a stranglehold, hoping their money will give them the security that only God can give. This kind of believer (yes, they are believers) lives with anxiety and stress, never knowing if God is going to come through when the chips are down.

I am sure Moses had believers just like that crossing the Red Sea (and they fill churches today). These half-committed believers crossed the sea, scared that at any moment either the walls of water would collapse and drown them or the chariots would overtake them and return them to slavery. Half-committed believers may have crossed the Red Sea, but there was no joy, no laughter, no peace—just fear. They obeyed because they had little choice, not because they trusted that the Lord would come through.

The other kind of believer is fully committed to the Lord and trusts that God will have the last word in all of life's challenges. They live with a sense of joy, awe, and anticipation of what God might do next in their lives.

Two types of believers—one filled with fear, the other with awe—crossed the Red Sea. One was filled with anxiety, the other confidence. Why the difference? It is the depth of trust they had for God. Prayer is a key element in developing that kind of trust. Prayer doesn't make the pharaohs of the world go away but gives us a way to deal with them through faith, peace, and confidence.

All believers start their walk of faith with a limited amount of trust in the Lord. Sadly, most stay there. Most believers pray, asking Jesus to change their circumstances, while in reality, we need not so much a change of circumstances as a change of hearts. It is when we truly open our hearts and lives to Jesus Christ with humility and faith that a new life begins.

John Stott, one of the greatest minds of this generation, wrote these words:[3]

---

[3] John Stott, in sermon: "The Greatest Invitation Ever Made," page 5. PreachingToday.com.

> Don't misunderstand this. This is not a call to copy the ostrich and bury our heads in the sand, and it's not a summons to murder our intellect or deny the importance of thought. It is simply to acknowledge the limitations of our human minds—that when we're seeking God, our mind flounders helplessly out of its depths, because God is infinite in his being, and we are limited and finite. Our little mind, capable as it is of remarkable achievements in the empirical sciences, is lost when seeking God. If then, we stand on our proud pedestal with our spectacles on our nose, to scrutinize and criticize God, we shall never find him. It's not only unseemly to treat God in that way; it's unproductive. If we seek God in that way, we shall never find him. If, on the other hand, we step down from our lofty and critical platform and humble ourselves before God, confess our inability to discover him, and read the Gospels with the open, unprejudiced mind of a little child, God will reveal himself. He reveals himself to those who, spiritually speaking, are little children.

Indeed, God is anxious to be known. The God of the universe so loves his creation that he came here; we are a visited planet. And we come to know God, not out of human intelligence or by strident legalism. We come to the Lord through humble, childlike faith, And as our faith matures, so should our prayer life. Through the power of the Holy Spirit, study, and prayer we can grow into fully committed followers of Jesus Christ. Our best prayer instructor is our Savior, Jesus Christ.

How did Jesus pray? In the pages to come, we'll examine the prayer life of the Son of God.

Chapter 3

The Six Prayers of Jesus

Prayer 1—A Prayer of Praise
Text: Matthew 11:20–26

THE FIRST RECORDED prayer we will examine comes from Matthew 11:20–26.[4] It follows Jesus's scathing condemnation of communities that failed to repent.

Matthew records what happens:

---

[4] Luke records this prayer a little differently than Matthew. Matthew records the prayer in the context of Jesus rebuke of unbelieving cities. In Luke's Gospel (10:1–20), he reports the sending and return of the seventy disciples along with the rebuke of the unbelieving cities.

> Then he began to reproach the cities in which most of his deeds of power had been done, because they did not repent. "Woe to you, Chorazin! Woe to you, Bethsaida! For if the deeds of power done in you had been done in Tyre and Sidon, they would have repented long ago in sackcloth and ashes.
>
> "But I tell you, on the day of judgment it will be more tolerable for Tyre and Sidon than for you. And you, Capernaum, will you be exalted to heaven? No, you will be brought down to Hades. For if the deeds of power done in you had been done in Sodom, it would have remained until this day. But I tell you that on the day of judgment it will be more tolerable for the land of Sodom than for you."
>
> At that time Jesus said, "I thank you, Father, Lord of heaven and earth, because you have hidden these things from the wise and the intelligent and have revealed them to infants; yes, Father, for such was your gracious will. All things have been handed over to me by my Father; and no one knows the Son except the Father, and no one knows the Father except the Son and anyone to whom the Son chooses to reveal him."

How often do we stop and praise our heavenly Father for the way he is working in the world? For most of us, the praise of God usually only happens while singing a hymn at church or if God does something out of the ordinary in our lives. In one of the few prayers recorded in scripture, Jesus praises His Father. Why?

First, praise reminds us who is God and who isn't. In my early years of ministry on Young Life staff in Tampa, Florida, I worked crazy, long hours. Part of the reason was that I loved what I was doing, I also loved those kids and leaders and desperately wanted them to know Jesus and be fully committed followers. So I worked seventy to eighty hours every week. Never took a day off. And for three Christmas breaks in a row I ended up in the ER with a diagnosis of gastroenteritis, which the doctor told me was a stomach virus complicated by exhaustion and dehydration. Later I learned gastroenteritis was a catchall diagnosis that doctors give when you are severely nauseous but the docs aren't sure why.

After the third trip to the ER, my Young Life supervisor took me aside telling me he wanted to talk about these emergency visits. Honestly, I thought he might praise me for my hard work; after all, the ministry was growing, kids were coming to know Jesus, and everyone was getting paid (which didn't always happen in Young Life). The ministry was thriving, but I wasn't.

He said, "Robert, the last time I looked at the cross, I saw Jesus on it and not you."

I was speechless and taken aback. I expected praise and accolades but got something else. Something more important—I got the truth, and he loved me enough to tell me. I had such a drive to be successful in ministry that I had gotten my priorities way out of line. I made plans and then asked Jesus to bless them. I worked those plans until I literally couldn't work anymore. Jesus wasn't in charge; I was. My motives were good and right; my application was a mess.

When we praise God, we recognize who God is: his character, mercy, and lordship over all life. And it was when I learned the power of praise; it helped me get my life in balance. Praising God for his plan and not mine has been a huge relief. Ministry isn't all about me making things happen. It is all about Jesus, who changes hearts and lives. Through praise, we are reminded to keep God front and center.

Another reason praise is important is that it not only keeps my eyes off *me*, it helps me keep my eyes off my neighbor. It's what is sometimes called the Silver Medal Syndrome.[5] This was first published years ago. In the study of Olympic athletes, they found that even though an Olympic silver medal ranks higher than a bronze, those who won the bronze were happier with their accomplishments than the silver medalist. Researchers discovered that all Olympians had sacrificed a lot of their lives to make it to the Olympics. Athletes of this caliber went to bed early, usually began training before sunrise and ate a restricted diet, and while their friends went to parties and had social lives, they trained. Any Olympic athlete leads a disciplined and sacrificial life.

I had a friend in high school who was a great swimmer. He worked hard to receive an athletic college scholarship. He

---

[5] https://www.psychologytoday.com/us/blog/goal-posts/201002/silver-or-bronze-medalists-who-is-happier.

was one of the most disciplined guys I had ever met. We went surfing one day. We both paddled out, but while I waited for a wave to come, he trained. Between waves, he pushed his surfboard as far away as he could and then swam to his board in an allout sprint! He was so committed to his sport that even when we were having fun, he saw it as a training opportunity. An injury kept him from the Olympics, but he did get a four-year scholarship to college.

All Olympic athletes are like that. That's what it takes. With such dedication to one's sport, I expected that all Olympians would have been excited just to make the team of elite athletes chosen to represent their country. It turns out that some medalists return home after the Olympics unhappy and unfulfilled. Researchers found that athletes who won Gold were happy, and the athletes who won bronze were happy, but the athletes who won silver were not and often lived with regrets. Silver medalist often felt that if they had only worked a little harder, or sacrificed a little more, or ate one less cheeseburger, then maybe they would have won gold. Turns out silver medalists focus not on what they accomplished but on what they didn't win.

We in America live with the Silver Medal syndrome. We have more in our country than in any country in the history of the world, but we feel like something is missing. On average, Americans see three thousand advertisements[6] a day telling us

[6] https://www.redcrowmarketing.com/2015/09/10/many-ads-see-one-day/. Some advertisers estimate that we see closer to ten thousand ads per day in America.

something is lacking in our lives. We see what our friends have, and we want that too. We hear of great vacations, and we feel like we deserve them too. We have great lives, great families, even a great God, but the Silver Medal syndrome reminds us of what we don't have. With so much, we lose our sense of thankfulness and our contentment.

One way to change our hearts is to do what Jesus did. Take some time (even during difficult times) to praise our Father in heaven for what we do have, his goodness, his mercy, and even what he is doing in our lives. Like our Lord, we need to praise our heavenly Father for who he is—his love, justice, and mercy, and when we praise our Father, we take our eyes off ourselves and our neighbors and put our focus back on him.

Prayer 2—A God Who Listens
Text: John 11:1–44

Have you heard the story about the old deaf guy who got fitted for two new hearing aids? They worked like a charm, and he hears better now than he has for many years. A week later he returns to the audiologist so the doctor can see how the hearing aids are working. The doctor asks, "Is your family happy that you can hear again?"

The old guy says, "I haven't told them, I just sit around and listen." He then smiled and said, "I have changed my will three times in the last week!"

My guess is that some of those family members would say that being heard is not always a good thing. But that's rare—most of us long to be heard; we want our spouse or best friend to listen when we have something to share, and that's particularly true about God. We want God to listen to us!

Does God hear our prayers? I think sometimes we pray never really believing God will hear us. I read about a community in Texas that was enduring a great drought. So the minister of the local church asked his congregation to come to church one evening and pray for rain.

When the members of the church arrived, the minister stood up and said, "Well, I am glad you are all here, but I must say out of this entire church, almost no one really believes God will hear our prayers tonight."

Some church members protested, saying, "We do to believe God will hear our prayers, or we wouldn't have come."

The wise old minister said, "You must not really believe because no one brought umbrellas."

How often is our prayer life like that? We say our prayers but don't really believe God will answer, and sometimes we doubt he even hears us. Jesus never wondered; he knew his Father always listened.

Or maybe we are like the young clergyman who was called to the hospital to be with an elderly church member who was about to die. He entered the hospital room to find many loving family members already there. He did his best to bring comfort to this hurting family.

As he got ready to leave, he asked if he could pray. They surrounded the patient's bed, and the minister prayed, "Lord, Mary is here lying in this hospital bed. Doctors tell us she only has hours to live, but Lord, you can do anything. So we ask that you heal her."

Suddenly Mary opened her eyes; she sat up in bed and said, "I feel like a new person. Praise the Lord, I am healed." She got up from her bed, hugged her family, and even hugged the young minister, who was so stunned he could barely return the hug.

Speechless, he left the now-jubilant hospital room quite shaken up. Finally, alone in the elevator, he looks up to the heavens and says, "God, don't ever do that to me again."

He prayed, but not like God was actually listening. He prayed, but not thinking God might do something miraculous. Sound familiar?

How shocked we would be if God answered our prayers in such dramatic fashion. So we pray with little hope or expectation that God is even listening. God is listening to every word. And even though we have no control over how our Lord might respond, God never misses a word offered in prayer.

Jesus knew God would hear his prayers. Jesus actually thanked God for hearing him at a dear friend's funeral. The story comes to us in John 11, where Lazarus (the brother of Mary and Martha) got sick. They were all friends with Jesus, so they sent a message to him to come heal Lazarus.

But to their consternation, Jesus didn't come for two days, and by the time he arrived, Lazarus was already dead and in the tomb. Martha went to meet Jesus, but Mary stayed at the house.

When Martha saw Jesus, she said, "Lord, if you had been here, my brother would not have died. Even now I know that whatever you ask of God, God will give you."

Jesus said to her, "Your brother will rise again."

Martha thought Jesus was talking about the end of all time, so Jesus corrected her by saying, "I am the resurrection and the life; he who believes in me will live even if he dies, and everyone who lives and believes in me will never die. Do you believe this?"

Martha affirmed her faith in Christ and then left Jesus to fetch her sister.

Mary came, and in her grief, fell at his feet and said, "Lord, if you had been here, my brother would not have died."

Seeing her pain, Jesus wept.

Many wonder why Jesus wept. He obviously knew Lazarus was going to be brought back to life that very day, so it wasn't over the death of his friend. I believe Jesus wept as he saw Martha, Mary, and their families grieving. Simply put, watching them grieve broke his heart. Don't miss this. We have a Savior whose heart breaks when ours break. We have a God who hears and who cares.

We live in a world where there are fewer and fewer deep relationships. Yet we long for community and for people who care. Recently, I ran across a news article reporting that an English company has opened named "Rent-A-Mourner."[7] So

---

[7] http://www.rentamourner.co.uk/ On their website they write: "RENT A MOURNER are based in Essex. We are available for funerals and wakes by appointment. We work with agents throughout the United Kingdom

if a loved one has died and you don't have enough friends and family to come to the funeral, for about $70 you can call this company, and they will send a mourner to your funeral. He or she will be briefed beforehand and will have enough information on the deceased in order to mingle with the other guests without being discovered.

Isn't that sad? Can you imagine having to pay an actor to pretend to mourn at a loved one's funeral? That is the world today. We all have many associates, colleagues, and church friends, but very few of us have close friends who will really listen and care.

Some of the best advice I have run across in a long time came from the writer Patrick Morley. He wrote these words:[8]

> Men, when our children were young, my business took off. My wife and I started getting invited to all kinds of business and community functions. But that meant shortchanging time with our kids. Patsy saw it first. I kept telling

---

and will supply a coordinator in your area to manage your needs. We are typically invited to help increase visitors to funerals where there may be a low turnout expected. This can usually be a popularity issue or being new to an area, or indeed, the country. We have a significant amount of mourners to call upon when the need arises."

[8] http://patrickmorley.com/blog/2015/1/9/prioritize-everything-based-on-who-will-cry-at-your-funeral; (adapted from "Part 2: Solving Our Relationship Problems" of the Revised and Updated *The Man in the Mirror* 25th Anniversary Edition).

> her, "We've arrived!" She said, "Yes, but at the wrong place."
>
> One evening, when we reviewed our calendar and a stack of invites, the thought came, *Why not prioritize everything we do on the basis of who's going to be crying at our funeral?* So we did it. This simple question—Who's going to be crying at my funeral?—saved our family. Why should you and I give ourselves to people who don't love us, at the expense of those who do?

Aren't we all guilty of that? We give our best to those who care the least and give our leftover time and energy to those who love us most. Then we wonder why we feel so alone in this world.

Years ago, the Speaker of the House of Representatives was a Texan named Sam Rayburn. He was told by his doctors that he had terminal cancer. Soon afterward he shocked everyone by announcing he was going back to his small town in Bonham, Texas. Many tried to get him to stay in Washington, DC, where there were great doctors and the finest hospitals, but he was determined to move back home.

When pressed as to why, he said, "Because in Bonham, Texas, they know if you're sick, and they care when you die."

We all crave community and love. There is no greater love than the gracious, awesome, pursuing love of Jesus.

Jesus is not some uncaring God, living distantly in heaven. Our text reveals a Savior who loves us so deeply that his heart breaks when our heart breaks, and he mourns when we mourn. Even more, Romans 8 tells us that Jesus still prays for us to this day. As believers, God has called us to love others like Jesus loves us. Romans 12:15 says it like this: "Rejoice with those who rejoice, weep with those who weep." That says it all.

Jesus first demonstrated the depth of his love for Martha and Mary, and the story continues. They all walked to the tomb. Jesus commanded them to remove the stone. Martha protested, saying there would be a stench after four days. They removed the stone, and at this moment the Son of God looked toward heaven and prayed (verses 41–42): "So they took away the stone. And Jesus looked upward and said, 'Father, I thank you for having heard me. I knew that you always hear me, but I have said this for the sake of the crowd standing here, so that they may believe that you sent me.' Then Jesus commanded Lazarus to come out, and he was alive once more."

Jesus's prayer begins with thanksgiving. Jesus says, "Father, I thank you." Now, in the last chapter, we saw how important it is to start our prayers with praise, and now we see that "thanks" is a second big part of Jesus's prayer life. After praise, Jesus thanks God for hearing him.

Do you believe God always hears you? Sometimes I get an immediate response to prayer, and at other times my request is met with silence. We are sometimes like Mary and Martha, who sent for Jesus, and for two days Jesus doesn't respond to their request.

Does it mean God didn't hear their prayers—or worse, didn't care about their sick brother? No, God always hears our prayers. As a matter of fact, God loves when we pray. Revelation 5:8 says that in the end times there will be twenty-four elders who will stand before Christ, and they will each be holding a harp and golden bowls full of incense, which are the prayers of the saints. Did you catch that? Our prayers are so precious to God that he collects them and they are like incense to him.

So why then does God answer some prayers quickly while others can take years? The writer and preacher Max Lucado, tells of a time when his oldest daughter was about six years old and they were talking together. Apparently, she didn't like the fact that he was a minister and author. She wanted him to leave the ministry.

"I like you as a preacher," she explained. "I just really wish you sold snow cones."

Lucado writes[9]:

> An honest request from a pure heart. It made sense to her that the happiest people in the world were the men who drove the snow cone trucks. You play music. You sell goodies. You make kids happy. What more could you want? I heard her request but didn't heed it. Why? Because I knew better. I know what I'm called to do and what I need to do. The fact is, I knew more about life than she did. Same with God. God hears our requests. But his answer is not always what we'd

[9] https://www.crosswalk.com/devotionals/upwords/upwords-week-of-january-25-30.html

> like it to be. Why? Because God knows more about life than we do.

God doesn't always answer our prayers quickly or always give us what we ask for—not because he doesn't love us but because he does.

There is one more prayer nugget in this text. Jesus starts his prayer with praise and thanks God for always hearing his prayers, and then he says something that might surprise you. Jesus said in verse 42: "I knew that you always hear me, but I have said this for the sake of the crowd standing here, so that they may believe that you sent me."

Did you miss that the first time you read it? Jesus said he prayed out loud so that others might believe. Have you ever thought that your public prayers are not always for your benefit but at times God might use public prayer to help others believe? Now I know we Christians have bristled in recent years as public prayers have been removed from sporting events and graduations. There is an ongoing debate about public prayer happening at the opening of city council meetings, rotary clubs, and other public events.

As our culture moves further and further away from our spiritual roots, this kind of formal prayer will most likely continue to disappear. But what can't be taken away are the prayers of individuals at homes, restaurants, hospitals, and workstations.

I recently visited a relative of a former member who was in the hospital. In that other hospital bed behind a privacy curtain was a roommate watching TV. I visited with my new friend, and we talked about faith and church, sharing what God was doing in our lives.

As I got ready to leave, I asked if we could pray together. We prayed for a couple of minutes, and as I headed for the door, the patient behind the curtain in the next bed asked to speak with me. I told him I would be glad to.

He told me he had been listening to our conversation and even our prayer. He then said, "Would you pray for me?" And we did.

I guarantee the reason he asked me to pray for him was that he had heard me pray. Somehow the prayer with his hospital roommate (a total stranger) touched his heart, and he knew he needed God in his life too.

What I am saying is that public prayers don't have to come over a loudspeaker to make a difference in someone's life. Just bowing your head and asking a silent blessing in a restaurant sends a subtle message to those who are watching, praying for someone in a crisis at your school, or praying for a neighbor in need. This simple act of faith not only invites Christ into a situation, that sacred moment can help draw a passersby to the life-giver, none other than Jesus Christ.

So in Jesus's second prayer, we see that he affirms that God always hears and values our prayers, and in fact, collects them in heaven. Jesus intentionally prayed aloud to be a living proclamation of hope for those in the crowd who might possess a flagging faith. Prayer changes everyone it touches, even those who may overhear or witness a prayer in a hospital or restaurant.

Prayer 3—Prayer that Brings Strength Text: John 12:20–36

I recently read a story[10] of a young soldier who messed up and was dressed down by his senior officer. The officer had gone beyond the bounds of acceptable behavior, even for the army. In fact, it was more like public humiliation than discipline.

Well, the officer knew he had overdone it, so he pretended not to hear the young soldier when through gritted teeth he mumbled, "I'll make you regret this if it is the last thing I ever do."

A few days passed, and their company found themselves in a battle taking heavy fire. The officer was wounded and cut off from his troops. Through the fog of the battlefield, he saw someone coming to his rescue. It was the young soldier. Ignoring the risk to his own life, the soldier ran to the officer and dragged him to safety.

Once they were safe, the officer said apologetically, "Son, I owe you my life."

The young soldier looked at him and with a smile on his face said, "I told you that I would make you regret humiliating me if it was the last thing I ever did."

That young soldier did make that officer regret his words. But he did so not by doing harm or getting revenge but through sacrifice, through personal risk through service to someone who had wronged him. That soldier had learned a different way of living.

---

[10] King Duncan, Collected Sermons, www.Sermons.com.

All through the Bible, we find Jesus calling us to learn to live life differently from the rest of the world. And in this text we see Jesus showing his disciples a new way to live. The story takes place a few days after Palm Sunday. The city of Jerusalem had been electrified after the huge welcome of Jesus with palm branches and cheers. Jesus's popularity had grown so large that he even had some special guests who wanted to find out who he was. This is from John 12:20–32:

> Now among those who went up to worship at the festival were some Greeks.
>
> They came to Philip, who was from Bethsaida in Galilee, and said to him, "Sir, we wish to see Jesus." Philip went and told Andrew; then Andrew and Philip went and told Jesus.
>
> Jesus answered them, "The hour has come for the Son of Man to be glorified.
>
> Very truly, I tell you, unless a grain of wheat falls into the earth and dies, it remains just a single grain; but if it dies, it bears much fruit. Those who love their life lose it, and those who hate their life in this world will keep it for eternal life. Whoever serves me must follow me, and where I am, there will my servant be also. Whoever serves me, the Father will honor. "Now my soul is troubled. And what should I say—'Father, save me from this hour'? No, it is for this reason that I have come to this

> hour. Father, glorify your name." Then a voice came from heaven, "I have glorified it, and I will glorify it again."
>
> The crowd standing there heard it and said that it was thunder. Others said, "An angel has spoken to him."
>
> Jesus answered, "This voice has come for your sake, not for mine. Now is the judgment of this world; now the ruler of this world will be driven out. And I, when I am lifted up from the earth, will draw all people to myself."

In this text, we find that Jesus's popularity is at an all-time high; even Greeks (non-Jewish people) sought Jesus. I am sure the disciples thought that with all this popularity, this was the moment Jesus would establish his kingdom on earth. This would be the time he would rally an army and run the Romans out of Jerusalem and Israel. Surely, this was the moment that God's reign would be restored in Israel.

But Jesus doesn't do any of those things. While the crowds are clamoring for Jesus to lead them and be their new King, he tells the disciples that he is going to die. Hardly a way to launch a new kingdom.

And Jesus is tempted here by Satan just as he was tempted in the desert early in his ministry. In this text, there is another form of temptation for Jesus, one that comes with popularity and fame—the temptation to abandon what God had sent him to do and give in to the popularity and to what the people wanted from him.

This temptation comes to all in public life. Do you remember who succumbed to that temptation within a few days of Jesus's crucifixion? It was Pontius Pilate. Jesus had been brought before Pilate for questioning. Pilate told the large crowd that had gathered that he could find no charge against Jesus. In fact, Mark 15:15 states, "So Pilate, wishing to satisfy the crowd, released Barabbas for them; and after flogging Jesus, he handed him over to be crucified."

Did you catch that? The reason Pilate had Jesus crucified wasn't that Jesus had blasphemed against God or broken a Roman law. No, it was to "satisfy the crowd."

How many of us have caved in to do something we didn't like doing but felt pressured, or we felt like we had no choice, or we didn't want to disappoint someone or some group?

I once had a meeting with a successful businessman, I will call him Bob. He was retired when we talked, but something had happened decades before when was the vice president of an international company, something that still bothered him.

He was asked by the president of his company to go to Miami and entertain one of the company's biggest clients. He took this man out for a fancy dinner, and he paid for the dinner with a company credit card.

After dinner, the client looked at Bob and said, "Bob, give me your company credit card."

Bob asked, "Why do you want my company's credit card?"

He said, "I am going to the dog track and will be partying for a while. I will see you in the morning."

Bob told me he felt trapped. How could he say no to one of the company's biggest clients? He knew it wasn't right, but what could he do? Bob knew that partying meant strip clubs and who knows what else? He was there to make a deal. He gave him the company credit card.

As soon as Bob got back to his hotel, he called the president of the company (Bob's direct boss) and told him what happened.

The president said, "It was the cost of doing business. Let it go."

It turned out this customer spent a couple thousand dollars at the dog track and then hit some strip clubs. The total bill was somewhere between $2,000 and $3,000, which was a huge amount of money back in the 1960s.

Bob told me he never got in trouble for this, but he always felt bad about it. He knew it was wrong, and he hated being used that way, but the pressure to close the deal and be liked by the customer was enormous and even encouraged by his boss. He told me that if his faith had been stronger, he might have done something differently. After more than twenty-five years this incident still bothered Bob, and how do I know? Bob was my dad.

How many of us look back over our lives and find that we did something under pressure that we now regret? Peer pressure isn't something that just happens to kids; it can happen to anyone seeking the approval of someone or some group.

And when Jesus was put under that kind of pressure, one

key thing that sustained him was his prayer life. This brings us to Jesus's four-word prayer: "Father, glorify thy name."

In Jesus's time of crisis, verse 27 says that Jesus was troubled to his very soul. Clearly, he knew he had a cross in his future, and he wasn't excited about going through that agony! Who would? So he prayed, but notice

- he doesn't pray for strength;
- he doesn't pray for faith;
- he doesn't pray for his enemies to be vanquished; and
- he doesn't pray to be happy or even safe. As a matter-of-fact, he didn't pray for himself at all.

In his time of crisis, Jesus prayed for his heavenly Father to be glorified. Jesus wanted everything in his life and even his words to glorify God. And that's a great example for you and me. And my friends, that's a different way of living life.

If you live life to glorify God, people will think you are crazy, but it will change your heart. If you live to glorify God, you will discover life as it was created to be, which happens in two ways.

The first is through worship and prayer. When we come together on Sunday mornings and pray and sing hymns, that brings glory to God. I love all kinds of worship styles, but let's be honest, no matter what the hymn or praise song or chorus is, if the song is there to entertain us then it doesn't belong in worship. Whether we sing contemporary songs or ancient hymns, they are not there to entertain us or somehow work us up into a spiritual frenzy. They were written to worship the

God who created us, a risen Lord who has redeemed us, and a Spirit that sanctifies us.

So whether you worship in a historic sanctuary or a former warehouse, if the music and prayers don't primarily tell of God's love, mercy, grace, and the cross, then we have not praised or worshipped God. All we have done is make ourselves happy with a little religious entertainment.

The primary reason for worship is to glorify God. That is something we learn. I grew up in church, and I have done seven years of graduate school (in theology and ministry), and in all that time there was not one course offered, not one Sunday school lesson in any church I have ever attended that taught me how to glorify God in worship. Sadly, it is what most believers learn on the fly.

But there was a time that churches did teach people how to worship and glorify our heavenly Father. Back in the 1700s, John Wesley wrote a lot of hymns, many that we still sing today. He also taught people how to sing these hymn in a way that glorified God. So back in 1761, John Wesley wrote these words:[11]

> Learn these tunes before you learn any others. Sing them exactly as they are printed here, without altering or mending them at all; and if you have learned to sing them otherwise, unlearn it as soon as you can.

[11] https://www.umcdiscipleship.org/resources/wesleys-directions-for-singing.

> See that you join with the congregation as frequently as you can. Beware of singing as if you were half dead, or half asleep; but lift up your voice with strength. Do not bawl [to sing too loudly], so as to be heard above or distinct from the rest of the congregation, that you may not destroy the harmony; but strive to unite your voices together, so as to make one clear, melodious sound. Sing in time … just as quick as we did at first …
>
> Above all, sing spiritually. Have an eye to God in every word you sing.
>
> Aim at pleasing him more than yourself, or any other creature …
>
> See that your heart is not carried away with the sound, but offered to God continually; so shall your singing be such as the Lord will approve here, and reward you when he cometh in the clouds of heaven.

I love that sentence: "Have an eye to God in every word you sing. Aim at pleasing him more than yourself, or any other creature."

So let's begin there. Praise in worship is not a performance but an offering. Praise is not about us but about the King. So whether it is a prayer or a hymn or praise song, when we extol who God truly is, we glorify him.

The second way we glorify God is through service. It is not

just what we say but what we do. Kevin Miller is a minister in Wheaton, Illinois, and he was preaching on this topic and decided to ask people on Facebook, "What makes it hard for you to serve other people?" They gave great answers, including

- "Serving is hard when it doesn't fit into my schedule or plan. Like when I want to go for a walk or take a long bath, but my aging parent needs me to sort their meds, run an errand, or simply be with them."
- "It's hard when their need seems endless. I don't want to risk helping/serving because I may get sucked in. Being swallowed up in the serving and not getting to be the me I think I am or should be."
- "There is such limited energy left after a demanding workday meeting our basic responsibilities (whether with young kids or in the corporate world). How do you balance the need for rest and self-care with serving others?"
- But his favorite was this one: the person simply wrote, "others."

Yes, serving others, especially those who don't seem appreciative, can make it difficult. But for the believer, Jesus doesn't give us the option. We are to serve, and when we do two things happen, God is glorified and second, we become more and more like Jesus.

I read of a guy and his wife, who came to follow Christ. The Lord put something on their heart that they thought was crazy. That was to help bring a waitress they had met in a restaurant to a relationship with Christ.

So he and his wife went out to dinner where this waitress was working, and they decided to leave a tract on how to follow Christ on the table. They also thought that if they left a big tip then maybe she would be more likely to read it. They had $50 in their possession, so they ordered less than they usually would and left a $10 tip.

They saved their money for another month and went back to the same restaurant. They asked for the same waitress, and this time they ordered only $10 worth of food but left a $50 tip and the same booklet.

They went back another month later and asked for the waitress. When she saw the couple, she said, "I read that little booklet you left last time you were here."

The couple tried not to show how excited they were that she at least had read it. She continued, "And I prayed that prayer to receive Christ at the end of it. Then I called my husband and read the whole booklet to him, and he recited that prayer too."

At that point, I said, "That's wonderful! But what do you mean, you called your husband? Does he travel for a living?"

Looking embarrassed, she said, "No, my husband is in prison. He will get out in two or three years. We both want to thank you for leaving me that booklet and being so generous. Money has been pretty scarce since he went to prison."

Over the next few years, this couple met with this sweet waitress, and the husband mentored her husband in prison. When he was released, they joined the couple's church. And it all began with a young couple who felt God call them to do something crazy, to serve a stranger, to sacrifice their once-a-month dinner out, and God did something amazing.

Service always does two things: it glorifies God and builds our faith.

What have we seen so far in Jesus's prayer life?

1. He prayed regularly at the same time and often in the same place.
2. He began his prayers with thankfulness.
3. He prays publicly to build the faith of others around him.
4. And today, we see he prayed that God would be glorified.

But there is much more, as we will find in the chapters to come.

Prayer 4A—The High Priestly Prayer Text: John 17:6–16

The fourth of Jesus's prayers is the longest one and is referred to by theologians as the High Priestly Prayer. Because of the prayer's length, we will look at the first half in this chapter and the remainder in the next.

To understand this prayer, you need to know its context. Jesus is within a few hours of his arrest and crucifixion. Maundy Thursday and the Last Supper had just happened with his closest friends. Jesus knows these followers are about to betray him and run away, so he prays with them, and more importantly, he prays for them. It comes to us in John 17:6–16:

> I have made your name known to those whom you gave me from the world. They were yours, and you gave them to me, and they have kept your word. Now they know that everything you have given me is from you; for the words that you gave to me I have given to them, and they have received them and know in truth that I came from you; and they have believed that you sent me. I am asking on their behalf; I am not asking on behalf of the world, but on behalf of those whom you gave me, because they are yours. All mine are yours, and yours are mine; and I have been glorified in them. And now I am no longer in the world, but they are in the world, and I am coming to you. Holy Father, protect them in your name that you have given me, so that they may be one, as we are one. While I was with them, I protected them in your name that you have given me. I guarded them, and not one of them was lost except the one destined to be lost, so that the scripture might be fulfilled. But now I am coming to you, and I speak these things in the world so that they may have my joy made complete in themselves.

> I have given them your word, and the world has hated them because they do not belong to the world, just as I do not belong to the world. I am not asking you to take them out of the world, but I ask you to protect them from the evil one. They do not belong to the world, just as I do not belong to the world.

When Jesus knew his followers were soon to be without a Shepherd, he calls to his Father for intervention. He shares his heart and soul on behalf of others. Sadly, most prayers are all about the one praying and not those in need.

I love children's prayers; they are honest and from the heart. But they are almost always about them. Take a look at these charming prayers from children:[12]

- "Dear God, I went to this wedding, and they were kissing right there in church. Is that okay?"
- "Dear God, thank you for the baby brother, but what I prayed for was a puppy."
- "Dear God, it must be super hard to love all the people in the world, especially my sister. I don't know how you do it."
- "Dear God, I love Christmas and Easter. Could you please put another holiday in the middle? There's nothing good in there now."

---

[12] https://www.k-state.edu/wwparent/humor/god.htm. Some prayers were sent to me by friends.

- "Dear God, I want to be just like my daddy when I grow up but without so much hair all over."
- "Dear God, is it true my father won't get in heaven if he uses his golf words in the house?"
- "Dear God, please take care of my daddy, mommy, sister, brother, my doggy, and me. Oh, please take care of yourself, God. If anything happens to you, we're gonna be in a big mess."
- "Dear God, if you can't make me a better boy, don't worry about it. I'm having a real good time like I am!"
- "Dear God, when my mom makes leftovers, do I have to pray for the food again?"
- "Dear God, please send me a pony. I never asked for anything before. You can look it up."
- "Dear God, I don't think anybody could be a better God. Well, I just want you to know that I am not just saying that because you are God already."

I love those prayers, but they were always focusing on what God can do for them. That's fine when you are a child and new believers, but at some point, as we grow in our faith, our prayer life must shift to include others. Prayers that are always about the one who is praying show a need for more spiritual maturity.

Here was Jesus, the night before his arrest and crucifixion, when he could have prayed for anything. I want you to notice what he didn't pray for:

- He didn't pray for their financial situation (even though that's not a bad thing to pray about);
- He didn't pray for their happiness (that's important too);
- He didn't pray for their families (again, something very important); and
- He didn't pray that the new Church would thrive (even though it is the bride of Christ).

So as Jesus's earthly ministry is coming to a close, he prayed that God would do six things. In this section, we will look at the first three things Jesus asked of his Father, and in the next chapter, we will examine the last three.

Prayer Request 1—That God Would Protect the Disciples from Satan

Jesus says in John 17:12 that he has guarded them up to that point, and in verse 15 Jesus prays: "I am not asking you to take them out of the world, but I ask you to protect them from the evil one." If you remember in the Lord's Prayer, Jesus taught us to pray: "Deliver us from evil." So twice Jesus tells his followers (and us today) to ask to be delivered or guarded from evil. If Jesus prays twice for the spiritual protection of his followers, shouldn't we pray that God would guard our family, our churches, and other believers?

I remember when our oldest son was about to go to kindergarten. We were all excited about the first day of school, but Lee (our son) had to ride the bus. I was pretty nervous about putting this five-year-old on the bus for a short ride to the school. Truly, my wife, Virginia, was cool as a cucumber; I was a nervous wreck. So I came up with a plan. I took Lee to the bus stop, and as soon as he got on the bus, I ran back to my house, jumped in my car, and followed the bus all the way to his school. Of course, I kept a couple of cars between me and the bus so Lee wouldn't spot me.

I followed the school bus right into the school parking lot. I parked and ran to where the bus let the kids off. I saw Lee get off the bus and from a distance, I followed him. The teachers must have thought I was crazy, first walking calmly, then ducking behind a wall or door when he looked my direction. Probably in today's world, I would be arrested for doing all that. Or maybe teachers are used to crazy parents of kindergartners on the first day of school.

He never saw me, but I saw him, as he walked the hall searching for his room. He never saw me, but I saw him when he got lost and went down the wrong hall. He never saw me, but I saw him when he talked to friends, He never saw me, but I saw him when he finally found his classroom and went inside. He never saw me, but when the tardy bell rang, I looked into the window in the door and saw him at his desk and knew he was okay.

I am sure all first-time parents went through similar things. The way I was there for Lee and later Dan (our youngest son) is a great picture of how God stands guard over our lives. My job as the dad is to guard my family even when they don't see me or know they are in danger. That's my job, and that's the way God stands by us. Even when we don't see him, he stands guard. Second Thessalonians 3:3 says it like this: "But the Lord is faithful; he will strengthen you and guard you from the evil one."

And knowing that should give us real peace in times of temptation and life's storms. The Lord is not telling us to look at the world through rose-colored glasses or live recklessly. But when we know that our heavenly Father is guarding our hearts and lives, the fruit of that is shalom (peace).

Prayer Request 2—Jesus Prayed for God to Guide Them

You know there is no shortage of people who say they can help guide our lives. One of the craziest I ever heard of is a woman who says she can give your life guidance by channeling Barbie—yes, the Barbie doll.[13]

This woman, named Barbara Bell, from California (no surprise there) was an architectural illustrator, and she operated the world's only Barbie channeling service. So for only $3.00, Bell summoned up the spirit of Barbie to solve the problems of her clients. Barbara Bell explains it this way: "I appreciate and understand Barbie. She has been forced to be shallow all these years, but underneath she's a profound person." (By the way, Barbie's last name, according to this article, is Roberts). Who would ever have guessed that a plastic doll has the answers to all of life's questions?

[13] Mark Roberts—http://www.patheos.com/blogs/markdroberts/series/how-does-god-guide-us/.

Psalm 48:14 has a different answer. It states, "that this is God, our God forever and ever. He will be our guide forever."

And God guides us through

- the prompting of the Holy Spirit;
- using other people; and
- the teaching of scriptures.

Patsy Clairmont,[14] the author of *God Uses Cracked Pots*, tells of a time her youngest son, Jason, had lost his way. She said Jason had two goals in life: to have fun and to rest. She writes that he accomplished both goals quite well.

But one day, when Jason had left the house to head to school, there was a knock. She opened the door only to see Jason standing there with his backpack and lunch box dragging on the ground.

She said in a firm, motherly voice, "What are you doing here?"

He bravely said, "I've quit school."

"Quit school?" Then she tried to think of some motherly wisdom, but all that came to mind at the time was "A stitch in time saves nine" and "starve a cold and feed fever."

They didn't seem to fit the occasion, so she asked, "Why have you quit school?"

Without hesitation, Jason said, "It's too long, it's too hard, and it's too boring."

[14] https://www.dialhope.org/sometimes-we-have-to-just-get-on-the-bus/.

This time she knew what to say. She shot back, "You have just described life. Get on the bus!"

That's my kind of mom!

But my guess is that Jason didn't understand everything his mom just told him. And she didn't take the time to explain every detail. Even if she did explain why she said what she said, a normal teenager isn't always going to understand a parent's guidance. Sometimes moms and dads have to ask their children to just trust them.

That's how we are to trust God's guidance. Sometimes we read things in the Bible, and we may not understand it all, and God is saying to you and me, "I will guide you, but you must trust me."

Prayer Request 3—Jesus Prayed for Their Unity

So Jesus prays for his disciples

- to be guarded;
- to be guided; and
- to be unified (the last thing we will look at today).

As someone who has pastored three churches for twenty-eight years, I can attest that keeping believers unified has never been an easy task. Some say a pastor's role these days is to be like a short-order cook or coffee barista. Congregants see themselves as spiritual consumers, and the job of the clergy is to whip up whatever the congregant wishes to happen. Of course, the unspoken implication is that if the clergy doesn't "come through," the spiritual consumer will find a new clergyman and new church that will.

I remember one family in one of my churches where I had built what I thought was a deep relationship with a husband and wife. I sat with the husband's mother most of one night as she died. When there was another crisis, I was the first called and walked with the family through the critical hours. Their kids were involved in the youth group, and their daughter often sang solos during worship.

Then one day they told me they were leaving the church. I was wounded, and I said, "I thought we were friends. I thought we were committed to building this church together. Did something happen that I don't know about?"

The wife replied, "We have stayed at this church longer than any other church in our marriage. Take that as a compliment. It's time to move on."

Did something happen that ran this family away? I discovered later the answer was no. I heard later they liked the choir director at another church better than ours, but that wasn't the core issue. The issue at the root of this problem was that they saw themselves as spiritual consumers, not covenant partners. So they left the church in the same way someone might pick a new restaurant for dinner. And when yet another worshipping body serves up Christianity in a way that fills their wants, they will move again.

Another cause of disunity is spiritual pride. One of my heroes of the faith is C. S. Lewis.

He was an Oxford professor when he came to faith. But after he began his relationship with Christ, he had no intention of really getting involved in a church with other believers. To be honest, he was a spiritual snob, and he wrote these words:[15]

> I thought that I could do it on my own, by retiring to my room and reading theology … I disliked very much the hymns that they sang in church, which I considered to be fifth-rate poems set to sixth-rate music. But as I went on, I saw the great merit in it. I came up against different people of quite different outlooks and different education, and then the hymns … were, nevertheless, being sung with devotion and benefit by an old saint in elastic-side boots in the opposite pew, and then you realize that you aren't fit to clean those boots. It gets you out of your solitary conceit.

Yes, we as believers are called to be unified, and the way that happens is making sure we see church membership as covenant partners, not spiritual consumers. We must not insist on personal preferences, but we always must look to Christ and his preferences.

When Jesus was about to be crucified, he prayed for his followers. He prayed that God would guard them, that God

[15] https://www.thegospelcoalition.org/blogs/kevin-deyoung/ten-principles-for-church-song-part-1/CS Lewis: "God in the Bos., 62.

would guide them, that God would unify them. If Jesus saw these as crucial elements in the lives of his followers, shouldn't we pray for these same things for our families, friends, and church?

PRAYER 4B—THE HIGH PRIESTLY PRAYER JOHN 17:17–25

It is no accident or coincidence that God wanted us to see and understand how Jesus prayed for those early followers. I believe this prayer, like the other five written in the Bible, were placed there to teach us how we should pray. The first half of the prayer had three important prayer elements, and the second half has three more.

The text is John 17:17–26:

> Sanctify them in the truth; your word is truth. As you have sent me into the world, so I have sent them into the world. And for their sakes I sanctify myself, so that they also may be sanctified in truth. "I ask not only on behalf of these, but also on behalf of those who will believe in me through their word, that they may all be one. As you, Father, are in me and I am in you, may they also be in us, so that the world may believe that you have sent me. The glory that you have given me I have given them, so that they may be one, as we are one, I

> in them and you in me, that they may become completely one, so that the world may know that you have sent me and have loved them even as you have loved me. Father, I desire that those also, whom you have given me, may be with me where I am, to see my glory, which you have given me because you loved me before the foundation of the world. "Righteous Father, the world does not know you, but I know you; and these know that you have sent me. I made your name known to them, and I will make it known, so that the love with which you have loved me may be in them, and I in them.

Paul Harvey was one of my favorite radio personalities, and he told the story[16] of a three-year-old boy who went to the grocery store with his mother. Before they entered the store, she said to him, "Now, you're not going to get any chocolate chip cookies, so don't even ask."

She put him up in the cart, and he sat in the little child's seat while she wheeled down the aisles. He was doing just fine until they came to the cookie section.

He saw the chocolate chip cookies and said, "Mom, can I have some chocolate chip cookies?"

She said, "I told you not even to ask. You're not going to get any at all."

So he sat back down. They continued down the aisles, but

---

[16] https://christianforumsite.com/threads/funny-christian-stories.12970/.

in their search for certain items they ended up back in the cookie aisle.

"Mom, can I please have some chocolate chip cookies?"

She said, "I told you that you couldn't have any. Now sit down and be quiet."

Finally, they were approaching the checkout lane. The little boy knew that this might be his last chance. So just before they got to the line, he stood up on the seat of the cart and shouted in his loudest voice, "In the name of Jesus, may I have some chocolate chip cookies?"

And everybody round about just laughed. Some even applauded. And according to Paul Harvey, due to the generosity of the other shoppers, the little boy and his mother left with twenty-three boxes of chocolate chip cookies.

Don't you wish prayer were that easy? Just fire off that prayer and things just happen and your prayers are always answered with far more than you ever dreamed. Well, that does happen sometimes, but in my life, prayers are rarely answered with miraculous and speedy answers. For me, prayers usually go on for many, many months, sometimes years or even decades. We all know we should never stop praying, but is there a right or wrong way to pray for others? Could it be that we are even praying for the wrong things? I think we can learn a lot by seeing how Jesus prays.

We saw in the previous chapter, how Jesus was just days before his crucifixion and he prayed for his followers to be guarded, guided, and united, but there is more.

Prayer Request 4—Jesus Prayed for the Sanctification of the Disciples

As we read on, we find that Jesus prays that his disciples are sanctified. Sanctification is the process by which God makes us more and more like Jesus. Romans 8:29 says: "For those whom he foreknew he also predestined to be conformed to the image of his Son, in order that he might be the firstborn within a large family."

First Peter 1:16 says: "for it is written, 'You shall be holy, for I am holy.'"

We are called to be conformed to the image of Jesus. That is something that the Holy Spirit does in us.

David Yarborough[17] tells the story from one of Max Lucado's books of a wealthy lady who owned a small house on the Irish shore at the turn of the century. She was also well known for pinching pennies. The people who knew her were surprised, then, when she decided to be among the first to have electricity in her home.

Several weeks after the installation, a meter reader appeared at her door. He asked if her electricity was working well, and she assured him it was. "I'm wondering if you can explain something to me," he said. "Your meter shows scarcely any usage. Are you using your power?"

[17] https://www.sermoncentral.com/sermon-illustrations/75304/david-yarborough-tells-the-story-from-one-of-max-by-bobby-mcdaniel.

"Certainly," she answered. "Each evening when the sun sets, I turn on my lights just long enough to light my candles; then I turn them off."

Yarborough goes on to say, "She tapped into the power but did not use it. Her house is connected but not altered."

That's where the disciples were at this time in their lives; they were connected to Christ—but not altered. And Jesus prays that God would now begin that changing process. And don't we want the same thing to happen in our lives and the lives of those we love? How many of us know someone that at some point in their lives, asked Christ to come into their lives but went on with their lives like it never happened, they never grew, never changed; they added Jesus on as an advisor but not Lord. They were connected but not altered.

It is the job of the Holy Spirit that sanctifies us. It is not something we earn or achieve. It is the Spirit that does it in us as we pray, study God's Word, and serve. The process of sanctification begins the moment we ask Jesus into our lives and goes on until the Lord takes us to heaven.

Our spiritual lives are like an iceberg,[18] which is almost 90 percent underwater. As the sun shines on the iceberg, the ice is exposed to sun melts, and as the upper ice melts, the part under the water moves up until it is exposed to the sun.

It is the same way when we come to faith and our lives are exposed to the power of God and His Holy Word. God first deals with the surface issues, the obvious parts of our lives that

[18] http://ministry127.com/resources/illustration/sanctification-demonstrated-by-an-iceberg.

need changing. And after God deals with that, a new layer is exposed, and he deals with that layer until it melts away. Then another layer is exposed, and that process goes on time after time until finally, when people look at us, they will see our Lord.

That's what Jesus is asking that God would do for his disciples. Jesus is asking God to make his followers holy. What a powerful prayer, and one we would be praying for our family members, neighbors, and even ourselves. This is a lifelong process for each of us. No one can rush the process.

Billy Graham is the most well known and loved evangelist the world has ever known. One day, Billy and his wife Ruth were driving through a long stretch of road construction.[19] The traffic was slowed by the construction and many detours along the way. When they reached the end of the construction zone, suddenly the pavement was smooth, and they could proceed with their trip.

A road sign caught Ruth's attention: "End of construction. Thanks for your patience." She commented that those words would be a fitting inscription on her tombstone someday, and that's exactly what she did. On her tombstone was no long list of accomplishments, just this "end of construction–thank you for your patience."

Ruth Graham knew what all faithful believers know. That sanctification is a rebuilding of one's heart and life by the Holy Spirit. From the time we begin to follow Christ we are "under

---

[19] https://www.sermoncentral.com/sermon-illustrations/19427/one-day-billy-and-ruth-graham-were-driving-by-paul-fritz.

construction." The Holy Spirit works in us to renew our thinking (Romans 12:2), to take away our selfish nature (Philippians 2:4), and make us more and more like Jesus (Colossians 3:5–14). Paul said, "I am confident of this, that the one who began a good work among you will bring it to completion by the day of Jesus Christ" (Philippians 1:6).

The psalmist powerfully illustrates the sanctification process by comparing it to the smelting process of gold or silver. In Psalm 66:10 (New King James Version). we read: "For you, O God, have tested us; you have refined us as silver is refined."

The way a smelter would purify silver was to build a very hot fire, place the silver nuggets into a bowl, and melt them. The dross or impurities slowly burned off until all that remained was the pure silver. The way the smelter would know the silver was pure was that he would look into the bowl, and if he saw a clear reflection of his face in the liquid, he knew it was pure.

What the scripture teaches is that what the smelter does to silver, God does in our lives. Sometimes the storms of everyday life, if we are teachable, will be used like that fire by our Lord to burn away our doubts, our character flaws, and our impure thoughts, and slowly, as the impurities burn off, what will remain is a pure heart and mind. So, over many years, when Jesus looks into our hearts, what will he see? He will see his own reflection. Have you ever met a believer and the words they used and their actions were so loving and gracious that you could see Christ within them? That's what sanctification looks like in my life and yours. That what Jesus prayed for, as should we.

Prayer Request 5—Jesus Prayed that God Would Give Them a Mission

The next thing Jesus prayed for was that the disciples would know their mission in life.

In verse 18, Jesus says: "As you have sent me into the world, so I have sent them into the world."

Stop and think about that for a moment. Just as God sent Jesus into the world, Jesus sends his disciples to us today. The disciples were a sent people, and so are we. Everyone here has a mission, and it is to make disciples.

The Church, the bride of Christ, exists for three reasons: to praise God, to be a hospital for the walking wounded, and to be a launching pad for missions. Everything else is secondary.

Neal Sadler, in his book *Pouring Our Lives into People*, tells of a time when he was in seminary and heard Billy Graham speak at a banquet. He writes that Graham's style was very different than it was when standing before the crowds at the stadiums where he speaks.

He wasn't polished or overpowering in his manner. But one thing stuck with Sadler. Graham said that if he had his ministry to do all over again, he wondered that if rather than preaching to the masses as he had done, whether it would have been more effective to choose just twelve disciples as Jesus did, pour his heart into them, and encourage them to do the same. Graham wondered to that banquet crowd if that would have made a bigger impact on the world.

God isn't calling the church to be filled with new Billy

Grahams who preach to the masses around the world, but God is calling the church to change hearts one person at a time. God is calling us to be disciple makers.

As a clergyman for twenty-eight years, I often wondered what an unbeliever would think of the church if he or she saw women and men who were so committed to Jesus Christ that our churches would lead the way in taking care of the poor, making disciples, and reaching the lost at all cost.

Sadly, in my experience, if we were to take a poll at our local churches in the states, what would the average person sitting in the pew say the church's mission is? A stronger music program, better sermons, a great fellowship among its members? My guess is that making disciples is way down the list.

Indeed, churches need a mission, and individually we do too. What is your mission? It has been said that the two greatest days in one's life is the day they were born and the day they know why. What is your "why"? Find your mission, and you will find your why.

Prayer Request 6—Jesus Prayed that God Would Help the Disciples to Abide

Jesus prayed for his disciples and God, in his great providential wisdom, had those prayers written down for us today. Jesus prayed that the followers would

- be sanctified;
- find their mission; and
- abide with him.

In John 17:24, Jesus says: "Father, I desire that those also, whom you have given me, may be with me where I am, to see my glory, which you have given me."

And again, in John 15:4–5, Jesus says: "Abide in me as I abide in you. Just as the branch cannot bear fruit by itself unless it abides in the vine, neither can you unless you abide in me. I am the vine, you are the branches. Those who abide in me and I in them bear much fruit, because apart from me you can do nothing."

You see, what Jesus is saying is that as long as we can stay plugged in to him, we can overcome anything. While abiding, we can overcome job loss, personal failure, or a health crisis. There is nothing that this life can dish out that we can't handle as long as we are abiding—plugged in to Christ.

But let me illustrate what most believers do. Imagine you are holding a power strip in your hands. We all have these at home; we know what to do with these things if we want to get power to something, we plug it into the wall, and the energy flows through the strip to the computer or TV or whatever we are trying to get power to. Now you can have a cheap power strip, or you can get one that costs hundreds of dollars. You can get power strips with all kinds of add-ons and doo-dads, or you can get the stripped-down model. But no matter how much they cost, how attractive they are, how large or small, they all have one thing in common—they don't work unless they stay plugged in.

Our lives are like this power strip, and Christ says we can only get power if we stay plugged in to him, but that's not what most people do. Instead, they take the plug at the end of the power strip and plug it back into the strip's own receptacle. Then we wonder why our life isn't running right. It is because we try to run off our own power. And then we wonder why our marriages don't work, or why our lives are in a mess, or why we struggle with priorities. It is because we are plugged in to ourselves. Jesus says stay plugged in to him, abide in him, and that's where we will find life.

My folks passed away about six years ago, and for two years after their passing, we dealt with their estate. While cleaning out some of their old files, I found an insurance policy on my mom, taken out in 1941 or '42, worth a grand total of $250. The estate attorney had been dealing with the life insurance company for months, and the insurance company asked for a second copy of Mom's death certificate, which states the cause of death. Honestly, she was ninety-four, had Alzheimer's, and no longer knew anyone. Her condition was so gut-wrenching that her death was more of a relief than anything else. Her suffering was over.

In gathering the death certificate for the insurance company, I glanced at it, which I had not done before. And there the doctor had written the cause of her death, "Failure to thrive." That happens when one's body is just worn out.

But the phrase failure to thrive captures what happens to many people spiritually. When we rely on our own strength to make it through life, eventually we wear down, and we no longer thrive. We hang on. We make do. We survive. Jesus is teaching that we can only thrive spiritually when we abide in Christ.

In the High Priestly prayer, Jesus prays for specific things for his followers. If Jesus, prays these things for his followers, is there any reason we shouldn't ask the same things of God for those we love? Jesus prayed that his followers would be guided, guarded from evil, be unified, be sanctified, have mission hearts, and abide—stay connected to Jesus. When we pray for these things to be in the lives of those we love—we are praying like Jesus.

PRAYER 5—PRAYERS IN TIMES OF CRISIS TEXT: LUKE 22:39–46

I remember reading a *Reader's Digest*[20] story a long time ago about a woman who had a favorite spot at the local zoo. It was an exhibit called the House of Night. It was a place where you could see creatures of the night that would crawl and fly about, but because it held creatures of the night, it was nearly totally dark. She said that one very bright day, she stepped into the exhibit and (of course) was instantly plunged into total darkness. Almost immediately (she said) "a small hand grabbed mine." A hand of a small child had taken hers.

Smiling in the dark, she asked, "And who do you belong to?"

In a very quiet voice, a little boy said, "I'm yours … till the lights come on."

When it comes to being in the dark, there are two truths.

[20] Story reprinted at https://www.sermonsearch.com/sermon-outlines/87453/the-hour-of-the-power-of-darkness-5-of-5/.

First, many people don't do so well in the dark. Second, we will all experience dark times in our lives. We will all experience some event that make us drop to our knees, experiences that turns our world upside down.

Certainly, Jesus was having one of those kind of experiences on the night he prayed this prayer. Jesus knew all along that his life was heading toward a cross. And here he was, hours away, in the Garden of Gethsemane, the crucifixion is imminent, Jesus life had gone dark.

So what does he do? He prays.

Let's turn to Luke 22:39–46:[21]

> He came out and went, as was his custom, to the Mount of Olives; and the disciples followed him. When he reached the place, he said to them, "Pray that you may not come into the time of trial."
>
> Then he withdrew from them about a stone's throw, knelt down, and prayed, "Father, if you

[21] There are some minor differences in the reporting of this event in Matthew, Mark, and Luke. For example, Luke writes that all the disciples went with Jesus to the garden (Luke 22:39). Mark writes that the disciples accompanied Jesus, and then Jesus calls out three of the disciples (Peter, James, and John) to stay closer to him as he prayed (Mark 14:33). Similarly, Matthew writes that Jesus took the disciples with him to the garden (Matthew 26:36), and then Jesus calls out Peter, and instead of mentioning the names of James and John, Matthew refers to the bothers as "two sons of Zebedee" (Matthew 26:37). Also, Mark is unique reporting that Jesus used the word Abba (Mark 14:36) to refer to his heavenly Father. Even with these very minor differences the prayers are identical.

> are willing, remove this cup from me; yet, not my will but yours be done."
>
> [Then an angel from heaven appeared to him and gave him strength. In his anguish he prayed more earnestly, and his sweat became like great drops of blood falling down on the ground.]
>
> When he got up from prayer, he came to the disciples and found them sleeping because of grief, and he said to them, "Why are you sleeping? Get up and pray that you may not come into the time of trial."

If you have ever had the joy of traveling to Jerusalem, you most assuredly visit the Garden of Gethsemane. What you will find is that it is not a garden at all, it is an orchard. Many have a mental picture of Gethsemane being like a lovely English garden, with manicured bushes, clipped grass, and stone pathways. Gethsemane is not that. It is an olive orchard, during Jesus's day and still today. Gethsemane was a place of business. You see, *geth* in Hebrew (gat) means "press"—and a press was a large five-foot-high square pillar made of stone. The word *semane* in Hebrew means "olive." So Gethsemane literally means press of olive, or as we would say today, an olive press.

Like today, olives were gathered in a woven fishnet bag and placed on a special stone table with a trough on one side. Then the geth, or press, would be brought down on this bag of olives and left there, sometimes for two to three hours. It would take that long for the olives to be totally crushed and every drop of olive oil was funneled away.

So Jesus, at a time when he was feeling crushed by the weight of what was about to happen, crushed to the point of anguish (and other translations say he was so full of dread, he sweated blood), it is telling that Jesus went to Gethsemane—the place of crushing. And in this time of anguish, Jesus turns to his heavenly Father.

Now everyone goes to God when things go terribly wrong. Even nonbelievers will shout out a prayer when there is a crisis. Probably the most used three-word prayer of all time is, "God, help me." My father and people in his generation called that kind of prayer "a foxhole prayer." And believers and nonbelievers alike say those words when in time of crisis. There is nothing wrong with that cry of help.

But Jesus gives us a better way; he gives us an example of how to pray during times of trouble. I believe Jesus did four things at the garden that can help us when our lives are deeply troubled.

Prayer Request 1—Jesus Kept Praying

First, even amid this crisis, Jesus kept his practice of prayer going. Luke 22:39 says: "He came out and went, as was his custom, to the Mount of Olives; and the disciples followed him." While in Jerusalem, he customarily prayed in the garden of Gethsemane (which is part of the Mount of Olives). And as his day of crucifixion was looming Jesus continued to do what he always did.

A proverb that we often taught at my last church was, "You need to be in a church before you *need* to be in a church." I would say the same about prayer. "You need to have mature prayer life before you *need* a mature prayer life." As simple as that sounds, it is crucial in times of crisis to have had a prayer discipline and to continue that discipline during trying times.

Not too long ago, I had a call from a woman (not a member of our church) who wanted to talk. She told me that nothing was working in her life. She was in a dark place. Her daughter had been killed in a car accident, her son was unemployed, her husband was unfaithful, and now her job was in jeopardy.

I asked her who she can talk to when things go bad.

She paused a long time and finally said, "There is no one else, so I guess I just go to myself."

I asked her to describe herself in one word, and she said, "Alone."

As believers, we know we are never alone. No relationship can grow without communication, and that includes an intimate relationship with our Lord. It simply can't happen without a mature, growing life. A prayer life that is so consistent, so much a part of my daily life, that when things go wrong (and hard times will come to all of us at some point in our lives), we can tap into that resource, go deep with Jesus, and draw on his strength.

Isn't that what Jesus did with his heavenly Father? It was that prayer time that prepared Jesus for what was to come. I want you to notice one very important thing in this text. When did Jesus sweat real drops of blood? When he was arrested? No.

It wasn't in Pilate's hall. It wasn't on his way to Skull Hill, where he would be crucified. Was it when he was whipped within an inch of his life? When he was nailed to the cross? No. It was here in the garden of Gethsemane, when he prayed.

If you and I had been at Gethsemane the night before the crucifixion and witnessed how Jesus struggled and prayed that his Father would stop what was about to happen, if we had been there and saw him sweating blood, we might have said, "If he is so distraught now, in the garden, what will he be like when he is arrested and crucified? Why can't he be like his three friends who were calm enough to just sleep through the whole night?"

Yet when the time for the test finally came, what happened? Jesus walked to the cross with courage and faith, and his three friends (who didn't pray) were the ones who fell apart and ran away.

What was the difference? It was Jesus's time of anguish-filled prayer that prepared him for what was to come. It was that time of prayer that gave him spiritual power and courage. It was that time of prayer that gave Jesus the strength to face the pain, humiliation, and horrors of the cross. On that dark night in Jesus's earthly ministry, prayer made the difference, and it will make the difference in our lives too.

Prayer Request 2—Jesus Brought His Friends

The second thing Jesus did was bring a few close friends with him. When our world is in darkness, we often need other believers around us. That's the power of a good church that rallies around us, and not just in the good times but when there is a train wreck. The fact is, many don't have friends we can count on. We live in a world of loneliness and isolation, praying that somehow we can connect with someone who cares.

I read a story not too long ago[22] about a grandmother named Wanda Dench who was texting her seventeen-year-old grandson, inviting him over for Thanksgiving dinner. What that grandmother didn't know was the grandson had changed phones and phone number.

So she texted this absolute stranger by accident and invited him to Thanksgiving dinner.

When the stranger got the text at first he was confused and didn't know who was sending the invitation. But they texted back and forth and finally the stranger realized that the grandmother had texted the wrong guy. That's when things got interesting.

The stranger was a seventeen-year-old named Jamal Hinton. Jamal had no place to go on that Thanksgiving, and finally he asked Wanda if he could he still come over for dinner. In grandmotherly fashion, Dench responded, "Of course you can. That's what grandmas do."

Somehow the story made it to some newspaper reporter who asked to interview everyone.

Jamal said, "I'm thankful for all the nice people in the

---

[22] http://www.preachingtoday.com/illustrations/2016/december/2121216.html. An Accidental Invite at Thanksgiving, Ethan Adams, PreachingToday.com; source: "Woman Shares Thanksgiving with Teen She Accidentally Invited," Yahoo News, 11-25-16.

world. I never met her ... and she welcomed me into her house, so that shows me how great of a person she is."

I have often wondered how the world would change if every Christian in every church invited one lonely person to dinner. Indeed, the epidemic of our age is loneliness. The church is the place where believers will find friends. But the church should be a place where there are men and women who truly love others and who stay when someone's world goes dark.

I have done many funerals over the years, but when it is a family member, it is different. When my mom died, we asked the minister of her church to lead the service. But when my dad died six months later, at the age of ninety-four, he asked me to conduct his service. So I prepared, knowing that it would be a very small service. The rule of thumb in planning a funeral or memorial service is simply, *the older a person is, the smaller the attendance.* So when we planned Dad's service, I figured it would be family, a few staff members from my church, and a couple of close friends. My dad's friends and family had either died or were too old to travel. To my surprise, about fifty people from my church showed up. Most had never met my dad and just wanted to show their support. It is a scene in my life I will never forget. In the painful times of life, Jesus wanted his friends around, and we need to do the same.

Prayer Request 3—Jesus Didn't Hold Back

The third spiritual lesson Jesus teaches us in this prayer is that he was brutally honest in telling his Father what was in his heart. In verse 42, Jesus says: "Father, if you are willing, remove this cup from me; yet not my will, but yours be done."

So many times we think that to tell God[23] what we are really feeling is admitting we have a lack of faith or even plain talk would be disrespectful to God. But God wants us to be honest and share what's really on our hearts. And you can see this all through the Bible. Read Psalm 88:1–3, 14–18 (The Living Bible):

> O Jehovah, God of my salvation, I have wept before you day and night.
>
> Now hear my prayers; oh, listen to my cry,
>
> for my life is full of troubles, and death draws near.
>
> [It goes on—I skip to verse 14.]
>
> O Jehovah, why have you thrown my life away? Why are you turning your face from me and looking the other way?
>
> From my youth I have been sickly and ready to die. I stand helpless before your terrors.
>
> Your fierce wrath has overwhelmed me. Your terrors have cut me off.
>
> They flow around me all day long.

[23] It is interesting that the Gospel of Mark states that Jesus referred to his heavenly Father as Abba, which is Aramaic for Father, or sometimes translated as Daddy. This word makes clear the loving relationship between God the Father and the Redeemer.

> Lover, friend, acquaintance—all are gone.
> There is only darkness everywhere.

Does that sound like someone who is afraid to tell God how he is feeling?

Let me whisper a little secret to you: God already knows what's in our hearts whether we tell him or not. So why is it important to share our hearts in prayers? Because of what that kind of prayer does for us.

Jesus begins his prayer by calling out to his Father. The word he used here for Father is Abba, which is best translated as Poppa or even Daddy. Jesus is coming before his poppa and sharing the dread he feels about the crucifixion. He was honest; he shared what he wanted to see happen, that the Father would remove the cross from his future. He told his Father what had him in agony and held nothing back.

Our prayers must be that honest too. Pretending things are okay in our prayer life, when they are not, are dishonest prayers. It is only when we get real and share our wants, doubts, failures, hopes, and broken hearts that we meet God in real truth. It is in that place of pure honesty that God can use that prayer to grow us, mold our hearts, and give us faith.

Prayer Request 4—Thy Will Be Done

The last thing Jesus teaches us is that when we pray honestly and passionately about what is going on in our lives, we will learn over time that God is thoroughly trustworthy in all things, even with the things that break our hearts. Honest prayer doesn't separate us from the Father, it does the opposite. It draws us closer.

Billy Graham once explained it like this:[24]

> I watched the deckhands on the great liner *United States* as they docked that ship in New York Harbor. First they threw out a rope to the men on the dock. Then, inside the boat the great motors went to work and pulled on the great cable. But, oddly enough, the pier wasn't pulled out to the ship; but the ship was pulled snugly up to the pier.
>
> Prayer is the rope that pulls God and us together. But it doesn't pull God down to us; it pulls us to God. We must learn to say with Christ, the master of the art of praying: 'Not my will but thine be done."

And in my experience, when I have gone through tough times, it is only after I pray for a while and really share with God the brutal honest emotions in my heart that I can say the words *thy will be done* and mean what I am saying.

Whose hand do you take hold of in the dark times of your life? In a dark time in Jesus's life he took the hand of his Father, his daddy, and did four things:

---

[24] https://eisakouo.com/tag/billy-graham-quote/.

- he continued to pray, as was his practice;
- he brought his friends as support;
- he was honest in what he was feeling; and
- he ultimately trusted God in whatever happened.

And when we do those four things in our storms, we are praying like Jesus.

Prayer 6—Prayers from the Cross
Text: Mark 15:25–39; Luke 23:34, 46

I read about a minister who was doing a children's lesson. He asked the group of children if they said prayers with their parents at night. One little boy raised his hand and said, "My mom prays with me!" The minister asked him "What does your mom say in her prayers?" She says, "Thank God he's in bed."

Is that really a prayer? I am not so sure. Whatever it was, it sounds like that mom was speaking words that were both honest and heartfelt. From the cross, Jesus spoke to his Father in the same way. It was a prayer that is, of course, heartfelt, but more, it is both surprising and comforting.

It is interesting that the four gospel writers wrote different parts of his prayer, John doesn't mention any of Jesus's prayers from the cross. Luke wrote down Jesus's prayer asking his Father to forgive those who were crucifying him and included Jesus's last prayer, that he commended his last prayer, committing his spirit to his Father. These prayers found in Luke's gospel reveal our Lord who loves so deeply that he prays for those who are crucifying the Son of God. When Jesus committed his spirit to his Father, we see an intimate connection with his father even to the very end of his life. Jesus chose to commit his spirit to God, but let us not forget that Jesus could have chosen a different route. He could have called down legions of angels and punished all those who had lied and mistreated him. He could have stopped the crucifixion at any time but chose to be obedient to his Father and pay for the souls of all would follow. The prayers written by Luke are truly amazing, and anyone who understands what Jesus did is simply awestruck by his love.

It is the prayer from the cross that Matthew and Mark include that is often misunderstood. This is a prayer where Jesus's words are profoundly painful and in some ways mysterious. I have dear friends who love Jesus, who simply believe what Jesus was going through on the cross is unexplainable to the human mind. Jesus on the cross is so amazingly gracious, loving, and astounding that the human mind cannot comprehend its depth. My scholarly friends believe that his prayer is impenetrable by mere mortals. Indeed, what the Son of God was doing on the cross, the payment for human sin (justification) and the reconciliation of the repentant lost is so amazing, the human mind has trouble grasping such love. Yet if this prayer goes beyond the human mind, why would God include it? If my thesis is right, and God arranged for six of Jesus's prayers to be printed in the Bible as a way to teach us about prayer, then we must dig deeper. Let's turn to the prayer as it comes to us in Mark 15:25–39.

It was nine o'clock in the morning when they crucified him. The inscription of the charge against him read, "The King of the Jews." And with him they crucified two bandits, one on his right and one on his left. Those who passed by derided him, shaking their heads and saying, "Aha! You who would destroy the temple and build it in three days, save yourself, and come down from the cross!" In the same way the chief priests, along with the scribes, were also mocking him among themselves and saying, "He saved others; he cannot save himself. Let the Messiah, the King of Israel, come down from the cross now, so that we may see and believe." Those who were crucified with him also taunted him.

> When it was noon, darkness came over the whole land until three in the afternoon. At three o'clock Jesus cried out with a loud voice, "Eloi, Eloi, lema sabachthani?" which means, "My God, my God, why have you forsaken me?"
>
> When some of the bystanders heard it, they said, "Listen, he is calling for Elijah."
>
> And someone ran, filled a sponge with sour wine, put it on a stick, and gave it to him to drink, saying, "Wait, let us see whether Elijah will come to take him down." Then Jesus gave a loud cry and breathed his last. And the curtain of the temple was torn in two, from top to bottom. Now when the centurion, who stood

> facing him, saw that in this way he breathed his last, he said, "Truly this man was God's Son!"

Besides the Lord's Prayer, this prayer from the cross is the next best-known of Jesus's prayers. If Jesus's prayer on the cross is nothing else, it is honest and passionate and reveals the depth of love Jesus had for the Father. You can almost hear the pain in his voice as he cried out to his Father: (verse34) "My God, my God, why have you forsaken me?" Most people aren't sure really what to make of this prayer. Did Jesus lose his faith? Did Jesus doubt God?

First, to understand this prayer we need to know what forsaken means. We all know what it means today as we have all felt the wound of a betrayal of a dear friend or family member. A time when we had given our heart to something or someone and the one who promises never to leave you, says they don't love you anymore. The one you gave the job to and mentored, that spoke untruths about you to your boss or the coach who recruits a young person to his or her team, only to leave when a better paying coaching job opens up. We have all tasted the bitter pill of being forsaken.

We would all like to think that kind of thing doesn't happen among Christians, but sadly, it happens more often than we expect. I have felt that sting of personal betrayal by a Christian leader. I thought we had a close and honest relationship, only to find it wasn't what I thought, and I was crushed. I felt forsaken, broken.

Had God forsaken Jesus? Had God somehow pulled the

spiritual rug out from under the Lord of Lords? Had Jesus discovered that his heavenly Father had ulterior motives? No, of course not. When we dig deeper and look at the original meaning of 'forsaken,' we find the word is defined differently in scripture. The word forsaken has other meanings in the original language. It comes from the Greek word *kataleipo*, and it can mean to leave behind, or left alone. So at that moment, when Jesus offered that prayer, Jesus took my sin and your sins, and every bad thing that ever happened and put it on himself on the cross. Scripture says in 2 Corinthians 5:21 that "For our sake he made him to be sin who knew no sin, so that in him we might become the righteousness of God."

At that moment of payment for our sins (justification), God the Father who is holy and righteous would not allow himself to be tainted by sin and turned away from his Son until the payment for our sin was paid in full. At that moment Jesus didn't feel betrayed or tricked; he felt alone. This experience isn't unique to Jesus. All believers, at some point in their faith journey, will feel disconnected from God but never abandoned.

One of the most encouraging stories in the Bible is the story of the prophet Elijah. God had groomed and trained Elijah in the ways of faith and obedience for the tough days that would come his way. That day came when Elijah took on the evil King Ahab and 850 prophets of false gods.

Elijah and Jezebel had never had a positive relationship. Jezebel was a follower of the Baal religion, a horrible, pagan religion of the day. To prove that the God of Elijah was the true God Elijah challenged the prophets of Baal to a duel. They each sacrificed a bull, placed the bull on an altar made of wood, and then the Baal priest called on their god to send fire down to burn up the offering. Of course, the 850 false prophets danced and chanted for hours but nothing happened. Elijah, strong in his faith in the God of Israel, called on God to send down fire, and God did as Elijah asked. The fire reigned down. Then Elijah called on the false prophets to be killed, and he rebuked the evil King Ahab and his queen Jezebel.

Well, this humiliation was too much for Jezebel, who swore that she would kill Elijah. Here Elijah, fresh from this victory, does not rise to the challenge, but now burned out, frustrated, and angry, runs for his life. God is faithful to Elijah and does not abandon him and sends angels to take care of him. Finally, Elijah travels to Mt. Horeb, ready to hear from God.

Elijah, at the end of his rope and scared to death of the evil queen Jezebel, hides in a cave on the side of Mt. Horeb. He felt alone (forsaken), his faith is drained, his soul is exhausted, and he waits for God to speak. There was a great wind, a wind so strong that it breaks rocks, and surely God would speak in the wind. But God didn't speak in the wind. Then came an earthquake—certainly God would be in the shaking earth, he thought. God wasn't in the earthquake. Then, fire came down, but God didn't speak in the fire.

Then the text says Elijah heard the still, quiet voice, a whisper, the sound of a breeze, and there Elijah heard the voice of God. Friends, God often speaks in whispers, but our lives are so filled with noise and activity, and regrets and pain, that we wouldn't hear God speak if he were sitting next to us on the couch. Mother Theresa said,[25] "We need to find God, and he can't be found in noise and restlessness. God is the friend of silence. See how nature—trees, flowers, grass—grow in silence; see the stars, the moon, and the sun, see how they move in silence. We need silence to be able to touch souls."

Silence is where we grow because in silence we can hear the voice of God. And Elijah heard God on that day. But Elijah doesn't submit to God's words; no, Elijah spews out all his complaints. He complains he was the only one in the entire country who truly loved God; he was the only one who was faithful; everyone else had forsaken God and the faith of Abraham. Indeed, Elijah felt alone in the world.

I am sure he was expecting God to have sympathy for him, and that God would tell Elijah how proud he was of him for being faithful and for vanquishing all those false prophets of Baal. But that's not what God did. God surprised him and told him to stop feeling bad for himself, that breaktime was over and to get back to work. God told Elijah he was not alone, there were seven thousand other faithful believers in Israel (verse 18), and his job wasn't over.

For all who have ever felt alone, even separated from God, that is not a unique experience. In those moments Jesus taught us to share our hearts with the Father, bear our souls in prayer, and we will discover that, yes, we at times may feel alone, but the Lord has us in the palm of his hand. That's what the scriptures teach us, Romans 8:38–39 says: "For I am convinced that neither death, nor life, nor angels, nor rulers, nor things

[25] PreachingNow.com, Volume 4, No. 12.

present, nor things to come, nor powers, nor height, nor depth, nor anything else in all creation, will be able to separate us from the love of God in Christ Jesus our Lord."

It says in Isaiah 43:1–3:

> But now thus says the Lord, he who created you, O Jacob, he who formed you, O Israel: Do not fear, for I have redeemed you; I have called you by name, you are mine.
>
> When you pass through the waters, I will be with you; and through the rivers, they shall not overwhelm you; when you walk through fire you shall not be burned, and the flame shall not consume you. For I am the Lord your God, the Holy One of Israel, your Savior.

In those times in life where we feel alone (forsaken), cling to Jesus and his promises, and like Elijah, the Lord, in time, will renew you and continue to use you to build his kingdom.

CHAPTER 4

A PRAYER LIFE LIKE JESUS

KEITH MILLER AND Bruce Larson, in their book *The Edge of Adventure,* tell the story of a guy who was traveling through the Nevada desert. His car breaks down, and he doesn't see another car for hours. He has no water, and he knows he couldn't just sit there forever, so he begins to walk.

He walks for hours. The thirst begins to be unbearable in the desert sun. He spots a gas station up ahead, and he runs there only to find that the gas station is abandoned. He looks around for something to drink and then sees an old fashioned water pump off to the side of the building. It is the kind of pump with a long handle that you pump by hand. He stumbles over and sees an old can wired to the pump handle. Inside the can is this letter:

> This pump is all right as of June 1962. I put a new sucker washer into it and it ought to last for years. But the washer dries out and the pump has got to be primed. Under the white rock I buried a bottle of water, out of the sun and cork end up. There's enough water in it to prime the pump, but not if you drink some first. Pour about one-fourth and let her soak to wet the leather. Then pour in the rest medium fast and pump like crazy. You'll git water. The well has never run dry. Have faith. When you git watered up, fill the bottle and put it back like you found it for the next feller.
>
> (signed) Desert Pete.
>
> P.S. Don't go drinking the water first. Prime the pump with it and you'll git all you can hold.

Now, let me ask you if that was you in the desert, dying of thirst, and you came upon this hand water pump and a letter from Desert Pete, what would you do? Would you drink the water and forget about the water pump, or would you trust Desert Pete and use the water to prime the pump and possibly get enough water to save your life? How do you make that decision?

I think the answer depends on what you know of Desert Pete. If you knew of him and knew he was trustworthy, you would probably try to prime the water pump. But if you thought he was some crazy guy who lived in the desert, you might not even want to drink the water in the jar. Your decision is based on how well you know him.

Our spiritual lives are no different. The point is this: *How we lead our lives and how we make life's decisions all depend on how much we know and trust Jesus Christ.*

Is our relationship with Christ ankle deep? Do we know of Jesus, or do we know him? If the world teaches one thing and scripture teaches another, which one will you trust? It depends on how well you know the Messiah. If Jesus is who he says he is, and I believe he is, then how well you know him is the single most important factor determining whether your life will be full of regrets and emotional scars or full of joy, purpose, and satisfaction. In short, many of life's most important decisions—like career choice, our marriage partner, whether we tithe or not at all—depends on how well we know the Son of Man. One of the most important ways we get to know Jesus is by praying. So for the rest of this chapter, I want to apply what we saw in Jesus's prayer life to our own spiritual journey.

1. Pray daily—Jesus's prayer life was regular. Faithful Jews in Jesus's day prayed at least three times a day. We find nothing in scripture that says Jesus didn't also practice that custom. But clearly there were other times of prayer, some of these prayer times some were short. The important thing is to set aside time every day to pray. I have my devotional time in the mornings. At least once a week I take what I call a prayer walk. This

is about an hour alone with the Lord in the woods, or on the beach, or at a park, just praying and walking.

2. Start your prayer time by reading scripture. I have used some devotional books over the years, but more times than not, just reading through a book of the Bible, a little each day, has meant the most to me.
3. Our prayers must be honest and passionate. But I have also found that if I don't have some kind of structure to my morning prayers, I end up being a rambling mess. Without structure, my prayers tend to fall back to me telling Jesus what to do to make me happy. So here is an acronym—ACTSIC—that I have used to structure my prayer life. If we want to pray like Jesus, we must ACT-SIC. Easy to remember, isn't it? Let's take that acronym apart.

   A—Adoration—We begin prayer with adoration. Telling God how much I admire who he is. How much his love, justice, mercy, and grace personally mean to me. Remember, God loves us so much; he not only hears us as we pray, he actually collects our prayers.

   C—Confession—Step two is confessing my fears, sins, and failures. Obviously, this prayer element was not part of Jesus's prayer life. But scripture is full of texts that clearly speak on the topic of sin and confession. Here are just a few examples:

Psalm 32:5—"Then I acknowledged my sin to you, and I did not hide my iniquity; I said, 'I will confess my transgressions to the Lord,' and you forgave the guilt of my sin."

Romans 10:9—"because if you confess with your lips that Jesus is Lord and believe in your heart that God raised him from the dead, you will be saved."

1 John 1:9—"If we confess our sins, he who is faithful and just will forgive us our sins and cleanse us from all unrighteousness."

T—Thanksgiving—The third step is thanking God for all he has done for me, my family, and my ministry. I express how thankful I am for his forgiving love and the many gifts the Lord has placed in my life. Jesus began his prayer for Lazarus by thanking his Father, who hears him.

Sometimes this part of my prayer life is anemic. Like many, I sometimes forget that thanksgiving is more than a holiday that happens in late November each year. Thanksgiving must be a regular part of a vital prayer life.

In his blog, Joe Carter writes:[26] "The one thing all humans have in common is that each of us wants to be happy," says Brother David Steindl-Rast, a Benedictine monk and interfaith scholar. And happiness, he suggests, is born from gratitude.

[26] https://blog.acton.org/archives/104831-why-gratitude-is-the-key-to-happiness.html.

Steindl-Rast explains why the master key to happiness is being grateful for the gifts we've been given.

Brother David is right. Being thankful is the master key to happiness. Yet, I confess I often speed through this step in my prayer life. I might list some things Jesus has done for me, but I confess I don't always think about just how blessed I am.

To remedy this temptation, I am embarrassed to report that I sometimes set a stopwatch to ensure I practice thanksgiving at least ten minutes each day. Recounting all the goodness I have experienced from my Lord and just being grateful keeps me humble and joyful like nothing else.

> S—Supplication—For me, this is my default prayer form. It is the time in my prayer life when I share my heart with the Lord on my needs today and ask the Lord to provide for me. I often time this prayer too, not because I speed through it (like thanksgiving), but if I don't limit my time here, I find I spend most of my prayer time on me and my needs.
>
> I—Intercession—I keep a prayer list in my Bible or devotional book that I use every day. I list my family by name and then list any others who need the touch of the Savior's hand. I list situations or challenges and pray for the Lord to enter in that situation.
>
> C—Church—The sixth element in a strong prayer life is to pray not only for our local church

> but the church worldwide. This is where we pray for missionaries and those being martyred around the world. This is the place where we pray for the church to rise up and meet the needs of the lost, the poor, and those swept up in natural and manmade disasters.

When I first started using the ACTSIC acronym, it was a huge breakthrough in my prayer life. It helped me to no longer focus my prayers on me but to have a broader prayer focus. After a few weeks of using the acronym, I noticed two things.

First, my prayer life came alive, and the second is that the time flew by. In my early years of following Christ, the idea of praying for more than a few minutes seemed an impossibility. I remember going on a twenty-four-hour silent prayer retreat as a young man. After praying for ten or twelve minutes, I wondered, *Well, how am I going to spend the next twenty-three hours and fifty minutes?* By using the acronym, I can sometimes go on a prayer walk for an hour or two and it seemed just like a few minutes. I actually prayed one entire morning and never finished praying through the acronym.

Here is how to begin. Plan to use the acronym and use a watch to make sure that you pray each category for two minutes each morning (total of twelve minutes). Once a week, go for a walk and, using a watch to keep time, pray each category for ten minutes (total of sixty minutes). If you can't think of anything to pray for, just be quiet and try to listen (remember, prayer isn't a soliloquy; it is a dialogue). Try not to focus on your watch, but use your watch to help teach you to pray through all the categories.

My prayer life today is nothing like it was in the early years of my faith journey. It continues to evolve and so will yours. I began as a new believer asking God for his favor in my life and to change my circumstance to make my life easier. As I grew in faith, my prayers grew in depth and regularity. Soon, I was praying for my family and for specific events and challenges in our lives. Now my prayer time includes not only my needs, but it includes adoration, thanksgiving, and silence—all spiritual elements that have come decades later.

My most recent changes have come as a result of my study of Jesus's High Priestly Prayer. I discovered that Jesus prayed far more specifically for those followers than I ever did for my family and church. By looking at the High Priestly Prayer, we saw six specific spiritual qualities that Jesus asked his Father to give to his followers. I have added these six elements to my daily prayers. I couldn't always remember all six so to help me, I developed another acronym—ALMUGS—to jar my memory.

Jesus asked his Father to help his followers to

A—Abide—that they would stay attached to Jesus;
L—Lead—that they would be led by Jesus;
M—Mission—that they would have a mission and mission heart;
U—stay Unified—that they would be part of a unified church/mission team;

G—Guard—that the Lord would guard them from evil;
S—Sanctify—that the Lord would grow them in holiness; in short, make them more and more like Jesus.

I want the same spiritual qualities that the disciples had in their lives for those I love and serve with. Again, using this acronym helped me pray far more completely for my family, my colleagues in ministry, and my church.

So now my prayer life has taken this shape:

A—Adoration—praising God for who God is;
C—Confession—admitting my sins and my need for a Savior;
T—Thanksgiving—thanking God for what he has done in my life;
S—Supplication—asking God to supply all my needs;
I—Intercession—praying for those I love that they might

A—abide in Jesus
L—be led by Jesus
M—have a missional heart
U—be unified with a church or missional body
G—be guarded from evil
S—be sanctified (made more like Jesu

C—Church—prayer for my local church but also for missionaries, martyrs, and the church worldwide.

Well, how about it? Are you tired of swimming in the shallow end of faith? Do you want Jesus to be more than an advisor but the Lord of your heart and life? A key part of that is learning to pray with honesty, heart, passion, consistency, and depth. Give it a try, and it will change your life and those you love. That's how Jesus prayed, and with time, the Holy Spirit, and an open heart, we can learn to do the same.

About the Author

Robert L. Morris, Jr. is a Presbyterian Clergyman and serves currently on the Young Life Staff in the Florida Region. He has been in ministry for more than forty years. He served three churches and most recently was the Senior Minister at First Presbyterian Church in Jacksonville, Florida (since 2000). He retired from First Presbyterian Church in Jacksonville in 2018 and rejoined the Young Life staff.

Robert has been married to Virginia T. Morris (an adjunct professor at Florida State College) for 43 years and has two adult sons. Lee Morris (and wife Katy) live in Puerto Rico where he is a photographer, videographer and co-owner of www.Fstoppers.com. Dan Morris (and wife Natalie) live in Mars Hill, North Carolina where Dan is the Student Activities Director at Mars Hill University, a kayak instructor, and a member of the ski patrol.

Robert graduated from the University of South Florida in 1975, earned a Master of Divinity (M.Div.) at Princeton Theological Seminary in 1986, and received a Doctor of Ministry (D.Min.) at Gordon-Conwell Theological Seminary in 1996.